John Patrick's Slots

John Patrick's Slots

by John Patrick

A LYLE STUART BOOK
Published by Carol Publishing Group

Carol Publishing Group Edition, 1996

A Lyle Stuart Book
Published by Carol Publishing Group
Lyle Stuart is a registered trademark of Carol Communications, Inc.

For editorial, sales and distribution, and queries regarding rights and
permissions, write to Carol Publishing Group, 120 Enterprise Avenue,
Secaucus, N.J. 07094

In Canada: Canadian Manda Group, One Atlantic Avenue, Suite 105,
Toronto, Ontario M6K 3E7

Carol Publishing Group books are available at special discounts
for bulk purchases, sales promotions, fund-raising, or educational
purposes. Special editions can also be created to specifications.

Manufactured in the United States of America
10 9 8 7 6 5 4 3

Library of Congress Cataloging-in-Publication Data

Patrick, John, 1932–
    John Patrick's slots / John Patrick.
        p. cm.
    "A Lyle Stuart book."
    ISBN 0-8184-0574-0
    1. Slot machines. I. Title.
    TJ1570.P38   1994
    795.2—dc20   93-45562
                                        CIP

To My Mom and Dad
and To My Daughters
Lori and Colleen

Thank You!

Contents

Preface

This book is on Slots. Can you imagine a book with this many pages covering a game as simple as Slot Machines?

My friend Paul Galkoski, who typesets all my books, finally stopped me or else I could have gone another two hundred pages. He told me it was getting too big.

But the biggest part of this book is not in its size, but in the Systems showing you how to play the Slots sensibly.

It all comes under the heading of Money Management and Discipline, setting Win Goals and Loss Limits and finally: Learning How to Win. That means quitting with a profit.

You got two choices: Pay attention to these Systems and have a good shot at winning, or ignoring the Money Management moves and playing like a dork.

The choice is yours!

Introduction to Gambling

1

Slot Machines

In case you picked up this book without realizing what the subject is, let me fill you in. The book is about Slot Machines.

We'll take an in-depth look into what Slots are all about, fill you in on the history and background of Slots, explain how they operate and then tell you to forget all that stuff.

Then we'll get into the real meat of how to play the Slots—it's called Money Management.

Most of you never heard of the term Money Management, but in the world of gambling, the whole difference in whether you win or lose comes down to whether you use Money Management or not.

But we're getting ahead of ourselves. There'll be chapters and chapters on Money Management moves that'll be laid out for you, but that section of the book is a couple hundred pages away. Let's move along at a slower pace, because right now you really don't believe how important Money Management is.

But you'll learn, you'll learn. And if you can finally convince yourself that it is better to win at gambling than just putz along like a dork, you'll use those Money Management moves.

Right now let's go back and start at the beginning. Let's take a look at the attraction of playing the Slots that capture about 85% of the people who enter a casino.

Maybe you'll see yourself as we fly through these pages. To be sure, you'll see a lot of your friends and neighbors.

The Slot Machine is far and away the most captivating form of gambling in the casino and maybe in the whole world of gambling. Take the Slots out of the casinos and the aura of the place would dip quite a bit.

Just remember what the purpose of this book is. It's to show you how to properly play the Slots. It is not my right to condemn or condone your playing them.

Naturally there are games that offer you less of a chance of losing, like Craps, Roulette, or Baccarat, but there are many of you who will just never play any other game but Slots.

You are the people I'll try to reach.

But way, way back in your minds I want you to stick this message and refer to it over and over again.

"Playing the Slots is all Money Management and Discipline." You remember that phrase and later on you'll see how it'll apply to your play. Slot Machines! The love of millions of people!

2

Should I Play Slots?

I get asked that question about a hundred times a day and my answer is always the same:

"I don't give a rat's tail if you play them or not. The key is how you play them!"

Then I always shoot back my own question in return:

"Do you use Money Management when you play Slots?"

That question is always answered by one of the following responses:

a) A blank stare
b) A stunned look
c) Silence
d) A quizzical frown
e) "What's Money Management?"
f) "Huh?"
g) A smirk
h) All of the above

If you are guilty of any of these responses when you question your addiction to the Slots, then join the millions of other players who really don't apply Money Management to any form of gambling.

I'll repeat this over and over throughout the book, so be prepared for it. It's none of my business whether you play the Slots or not. It is my business to make you realize how to

3

maximize your chances of deriving a profit from them.

To begin, let's analyze why you play the Slots in the first place:

a) You're scared to play Roulette.

b) You're intimidated by Craps.

c) You think Baccarat is a dance step invented by a French stripper.

d) You're too lazy to learn how to count cards in Blackjack.

e) You think slots is a chance to win a quick jackpot.

f) You think nobody will notice you playing slots and pick up on the fact you don't know anything about table games.

g) You actually like the thrill of playing slots.

h) All of the above, especially the "scared to be seen" factor.

Okay, you know darn well that you fit into one of those categories, maybe two or three of them and don't or won't change.

That's your choice. Just realize that there is a reason you play Slots and it is my humble opinion that most of you just haven't taken the time to learn the table games. A pity, 'cause they're snap city to grasp.

But let's stay with the game of slot playing. If that's to be your outlet in the casino, let's at least refine your approach.

In a nutshell, the answer to the question of whether you should play the Slots lies in your mind. You wanna play them, go ahead! But at least play them intelligently.

And that's what I'll show you. Will you listen and follow the rules I lay out?

No way, Jose!

Oh, you'll agree that the Theories have merit, but you'll be too stubborn to adopt the strict disciplined approaches.

But someday you'll realize I don't speak with forked tongue. Someday!

3

Reality of Slots

Let's put something on the table right now that has to do with the reality of gambling and especially how it pertains to the most popular game in the casino—Slots.

First of all, you gotta realize that the things I tell you about gambling are aimed at the "guy in the street," the regulars who pour their money into the casinos in the hopes of bringing home the windfall that will change their lives.

And I ain't talking about our neighbor, my friend, I'm talking about you! You with the short Bankroll and big dreams, who think on the days you win you're a genius and the days you lose God hates you.

Well, that's a lot of crap. You lose because you play like dorks and then blame everyone in the county except the person who peers back at you every day from your bathroom mirror.

There are two things to grasp from today's message and it has to do with two words I used back in the early part of this article. The two words are Bankroll and Reality.

Most of you have neither and 90% of you don't even know what these words mean.

Let's start with Bankroll, the thing that determines how much you will win or lose on a given day.

Bankroll does not mean $8,000 or $5,000 or even $600. Bankroll is the amount of money you take to a casino.

If you have $200, that's your bankroll. If you have $100, that's your bankroll. If you have $50, that's your bankroll.

Everyone's Bankroll is different, so if you are short on money in the casino, don't go walking around depressed—just adjust the amount of your goal to coincide with the amount of that Bankroll.

A guy with $500 to take to the slots should win more than the guy with $50 but that's because he has staying power. He can last longer at the machines.

By the same token, the guy with the $50 stake should not think he has the right to win as much as the guy with bigger bucks.

The amount of your return is based on a percentage of your stakes. If Bill Bucks can win 20% of $500 for a $100 return, he has had a great day. And if his brother Les Bucks wins more often, say 40% with his $50 stake, then he should be happy with his $20 profit.

But do you think he is? Don't be sil! That dork wants to double his money and won't even accept twice as good a percentage as his higher-heeled brother.

Which leads us to the Reality of gambling, the second of the two words that most people don't grasp.

The Reality of gambling is that your chances of winning are never better than 50–50. I don't give a rat's tail how good you are, your chances never get better than 50–50.

So if you win 20% of what you take to the casino, you're a roaring genius. If you won't accept that 20%, you're a hopeless dork, and that's Reality, my friend—something most people don't realize.

4

Can I Win at the Slots?

People have been losing at gambling for years and years. Billions of dollars are spent on gambling, whether it be Slots, Craps, Blackjack, Poker, Sports, Horse Racing, Baccarat, Lottery, Bingo or just pitching pennies in the street.

The reason people lose is not because the game is unbeatable, it's because the people who bet on that particular game are dorks.

They may be successful in business, in running a family, in making investments or in a thousand other enterprises. But when it comes to gambling they exhibit all the restraint of a runaway buffalo in a china shop. They don't quit until they break themselves.

For some reason, most people look upon gambling as a way to make a killing. That's garbage. In gambling you never ever have a better than 50–50 chance of winning, so how can you logically hope to double your money playing at something when your chances of winning in the first place are always less than 50–50.

I'll go over that previous paragraph in depth in an upcoming chapter but at least let the message sink in.

I'm not telling you that you can't win at Slots, or for that reason any form of gambling. What I am trying to make you realize is that winning means leaving the casino with more money than you brought with you.

If you bring $100 to the casino, play the slots for five minutes or five hours, and leave with $110, you are a winner.

The amount of the profit is not the barometer of the exercise. The fact that you did not lose any money should be your primary satisfaction.

The amount of the profit may not be what you wanted it to be, but then the guy who goes in with $1,000 and wins $100 is also probably not satisfied either.

Sure, the $100 would feel good to you, 'cause you started with only $100, but to him it leaves the same bad taste as you winning $10 with $100.

Sure, you can win at the Slots. Maybe not the billions you dream about, but you can leave with more than you started with.

But you gotta *wanna* win.

5

Naked Pulls

We're in the initial section of the book and you're not even close yet to getting the Systems and Money Management moves that will be part of your day at the slots.

But I just wanna jump ahead and give you an insight into what you DON'T know about gambling. I've picked a move called Naked Pulls. This will be explained deeper later on but I just wanna give you a taste of it now, because it's gonna be so much a part of your play.

Take a second right now and see if you can figure out what it means. A hint: the explanation is as clear as the title indicates.

Naked Pulls merely means nothing positive has happened when you pulled that handle for a number of plays. Naked means nothing and nothing has happened. So why stay at that cold machine?

When you go up to a Slot Machine, you should set an amount of pulls that give you nothing in return for your efforts. Suppose you pick the number 8. If you have eight straight pulls where you get zero coins back...leave that machine. There were 8 (or whatever number you picked up to 14) Naked Pulls, so obviously that machine is cold. Leave it!

Do you set Naked Pulls? We'll go deeper into this very soon, but I just wanted to make you aware of the things we'll be going over.

I've put it in the first section to get you to put your thinking caps on. We'll go over this again, but get your mind into moves you didn't think of before. All these little things will be part of the overall approach that will minimize losses and take advantage of streaks.

6

The Big Four

This is the last chapter in the introductory part of the book that will give you an insight into playing Slots.

The next four sections will each cover one part of the Big 4 in gambling. It is imperative that you have every one of these things in mind to have a chance of winning.

You should know by now what the Big 4 is:

1) Bankroll.
2) Knowledge of the Game.
3) Money Management.
4) Discipline.

Even if you know all of the above, your chances of winning is still only 50–50. So can you imagine how bad off you'd be if you lacked three or even two of the Big 4?

There are people who lack all 4. They may as well send the money to the casino for all the chance they have of winning.

Bankroll

This is where it begins: This is where it starts. You set aside an amount of money that you will bring to battle and that money is called your Bankroll.

You can't take a short Bankroll to battle or else your every move will be affected. But the money you do take is your own

Bankroll. It could be $100 or $300 or $3,000. Whatever the amount, that keys the bets you will make.

Knowledge of the Game

You gotta be perfect in the game you play. I didn't say good or pretty good or even very good. I said you gotta be PERFECT GOOD and don't think that because you're playing Slots, there isn't a bushel of things to know. There are plenty of things to fill your head and they'll help in teaching you how to win.

Money Management

The absolute necessity to successful gambling. MONEY MANAGEMENT is simply "What do you bet when you Win! What do you bet when you lose." Sounds simple, doesn't it? Well, if you have Money Management, you got a leg up on being a winner. If you don't got Money Management, you may as well use your leg to kick yourself in the butt for not having it. We'll be going deep, deeper, and deepest into Money Management in that particular section.

Discipline

And then we get to the meat of gambling. It's Discipline and it takes a lot of guts to exploit Discipline in the casino. Most people can't even spell it, let along practice it. But the day you get Discipline, your whole world of gambling will change. I guarantee you won't go back to your silly way of playing.

There you have the Big 4. Again I emphasize that if you lack even one of them, you're gonna get whacked.

The next section starts the real journey to being a winner. But go over this section again and get a feel as to what gambling is all about.

It's about being a winner!

The Bankroll

1

The Start

Now we start breaking down your day, laying out all the things you need to have a 50–50 chance of coming home a winner.

The obvious place to start is with your Bankroll, the money you will take to the casino. Since we're covering the Slots, we'll be talking to people who will allocate a smaller amount of money to their play.

In the matter of playing the table games, such as Craps, Blackjack, Roulette and Baccarat, a larger Bankroll is required. That's because the table minimums are higher.

In these cases, you should have 30 times the amount of the table minimum. That means that on a $5 Blackjack table you would need $150 per table and a minimum of 3 tables for a $450 Bankroll.

Craps has a variation approach. For the game you should have 10 times the amount of your initial bet. So if you played $5 Pass Line with $5 odds and placed the six and eight for $6 each, your lay-out would be $22. You should have $220 for that table or Session, again with a minimum of 3 tables, or a Bankroll of $660.

You can see that each table has its own set of rules toward the amount of money required, plus a logical way of distributing that Bankroll.

The reason you set amounts of money for each table, or in the case of Slots, for each machine, is to avoid losing all of your Bankroll at any one cold table or Slot Machine. This will also be covered in detail so don't worry about it just yet.

Just understand that every single move you make will be pre-determined ahead of time and no deviation allowed.

But it will begin with your Bankroll and that is the amount of money that you yourself set aside to gamble with on that particular day.

How much is a Slots Bankroll? Let's list some figures and you pick the amount that fits your budget.

1) $100
2) $200
3) $300
4) $500
5) $600
6) $1,000
7) $1,500
8) $1,800

Somewhere in that list is an amount that zeros in on your situation, and the amount of your Bankroll automatically tells you the value machine you can play.

Lotta Kash has a lot of cash in her kick so her starting Bankroll is $1,500 and she has a wide variety of machines to play at.

Her options range from the 25¢ Slots all the way through 50¢, $1.00 and $5.00 Slots. That's because she has the staying power of a large Bankroll.

Lee Tilshort is a little short on cash and his Bankroll for the day is $100. There is no reason for Lee Tilshort to feel embarrassed because of his lack of funds but it is imperative that he realize that his short Bankroll restricts him to play only at the 5¢ or 25¢ machines.

As usual, the human element of greed enters into most

people in the casino and Lee Tilshort is now upset because he wants to play at the dollar machines and take a shot at winning $10,000.

Mistake #1. His Bankroll has already signaled him that he is no higher than a quarter player. Period!

Methinks many of you players with a $100 Bankroll are having problems right now accepting this restriction, but that's the way the Ding Dongs.

You wanna play at higher machines, bring more money. If you can't bring more money, play where your Bankroll will afford you to. This will allow you to compete sensibly, while you wait for a streak to materialize.

Lotta Kash has the bread to last a long time at the machines. It doesn't mean she's gonna risk her whole Bankroll, but at least she can lose $50 and not feel the heat.

If Lee Tilshort goes to a dollar machine and drops $40, he starts sweating beads of despair 'cause he has five more hours to kill in the casino and only a handful of money left to do battle.

Bankroll, the amount of money you take to the casino. It's the first step on your journey. It requires you to set aside a certain amount of money per Session and DEMANDS that you stay within those parameters.

2

Sessions

Okay, you've settled on your Bankroll, and now you're ready to head to the casino.

I'm gonna say $200 is the amount of your Bankroll for this day and the examples will be based on that preset $200.

I know, I know, I know a lot of you are already complaining that your allotted money has never been more than $100 and that I'm talking over your heads.

On the other side, we have the higher heeled player who brings $500 or more.

Just adjust the Theory that I use for the $200 amount and apply it to your Bankroll. The Theory will be exactly the same, only the amounts will differ.

You're heading toward the casino, $200 clutched in your clammy hands and dreams of paying the rent, phone bill, car payment and dinner on the town running rampant through your mind.

Nice dreams, a little far-fetched perhaps, but at least it keeps your brain active as you head to battle.

What your brain should be doing is zeroing in on your approach to the day's business and how you will allocate that day's money.

Two hundred dollars has a lot of sock in the real world of living, but in the glossy world of gambling, it is a mere pittance.

It's a lot of money for Shorty Shortkash, who is already two months behind in his alimony payments and he looks upon the deuce to pad his wallet and win enough to put his ex-mate's dowry in her hand for the next six months.

On the other hand, Igott Bredd makes a $200 bet every 30 seconds, so that kind of cash is merely pin money for him.

It merely reinforces what I said about your own personal Bankroll determining your play.

Igott Bread has the bread to bet big, while Shorty Shortkash has to accept his lesser Bankroll and play within his stake.

It ain't gonna be easy for you to accept this, but you gotta.

Upon entering the casino you gotta make sure you don't bring the entire $200 to the first machine. A cold streak will eat into your money and if it doesn't wipe you out, it will at least leave you bloodied and bowed.

What I want you to do is break your Bankroll into Sessions. A Session consists of an equal portion of your Bankroll. It doesn't matter how much you bring to the Sessions, only that you have the intelligence to split that Bankroll into equal Sessions.

Here are some examples for $200 staked players:
1) 4 Sessions of $50.00 each.
2) 5 Sessions of $40.00 each.
3) 8 Sessions of $25.00 each.
4) 10 Sessions of $20.00 each.
5) 12 Sessions of $16.50 each.
6) 15 Sessions of $13.50 each.
7) 20 Sessions of $10.00 each.
8) 25 Sessions of $ 8.00 each.
9) 40 Sessions of $ 5.00 each.

A Session is a machine. Notice (7) for example, where you break the $200 into 20 Sessions of $10 each. You got yourself a shot at 20 different machines. Think about it!

Many of you have antiquated ideas about machines "due" to hit or "due" to stop hitting and that nonsense is strictly illogical.

We'll go over all of that later but right now I want you to zero in on the method of breaking that Bankroll into separate machines, or "Sessions."

The next chapter gives you variations of breakdowns, so you don't have to tax your brain laying out combinations.

Incidentally, with a $200 Bankroll, my choice would be (7) Twenty Sessions of $10 each or (8) Twenty-five Sessions of $8 each. That gives you a decent stake at a lot of different machines.

3

Variations of Sessions

The previous chapter explained what a Session was and showed an example for handling a $200 Bankroll.

We'll go over two more sized Bankrolls to give you a bird's eye view of how to look at this Theory:

Start with a $100 Bankroll. Break into:

(A) Three Sessions of $33.50 each.

(B) Four Sessions of $25.00 each.

(C) Five Sessions of $20.00 each.

(D) Six Sessions of $16.50 each.

(E) Eight Sessions of $12.50 each.

(F) Ten Sessions of $10.00 each.

(G) Twelve Sessions of $8.30 each.

(H) Fifteen Sessions of $6.60 each.

(I) Twenty Sessions of $5.00 each.

For the $100 Bankroll, there are fewer variables, but my choice would be (F) Ten Sessions at $10 each or (G) Twelve Sessions at $8.30 each.

However, if you like, go to (I) where you have twenty pops at $5.00 each. Your Session money is smaller but you pick up some extra machines where you can search for a hot Trend.

Let's swing over to you people who have a higher Bankroll and we'll pick the amount of $600 as the money to be allocated to the Slots:

19

(A) Three Sessions of $200 each.

(B) Four Sessions of $150 each.

(C) Five Sessions of $120 each.

(D) Six Sessions of $100 each.

(E) Eight Sessions of $75 each.

(F) Ten Sessions of $60 each.

(G) Twelve Sessions of $50 each.

(H) Fifteen Sessions of $40 each.

(I) Twenty Sessions of $30 each.

(J) Twenty Five Sessions of $24 each.

(K) Thirty Sessions of $20 each.

(L) Forty Sessions of $15 each.

(M) Fifty Sessions of $12 each.

(N) Sixty Sessions of $10 each.

(O) One Hundred Sessions of $6 each.

Notice that the higher Bankroll allows for more choices in the amount of machines you can attack. Just because you do have a higher stake of $600, that doesn't rule out the possibility of dividing it into multiple Sessions, such as (M) which allows fifty Sessions of $12 each.

One thing you should be aware of and I touched on it briefly. The amount of your Bankroll determines the value machine you can play at. Obviously a $100 or $200 Bankroll demands only a 25¢ machine but with a $600 Bankroll:

(1) You decide on the type machine you wanna play at, either 25¢, 50¢, or $1.00.

(2) You adjust your Sessions to that particular machine.

Let's say you wanna play at the dollar Slots. I would then go to (F), for example, where I can get ten Sessions at $60 each. Or you may opt for (D), where you have six Sessions of $100 each. That way you can play comfortably, with an adequate starting Session amount.

Naturally the same thinking would prevail at the 50¢ machine, where you could for example choose (I), twenty Sessions of $30 each. That way you have multiple machines and a decent working stake.

Even if you wanted to use the $600 Slot Bankroll at the quarter machines, you could choose from any number of examples.

If you chose (E), you'd have eight Sessions of $75 each, which gives you a lot of play at a few machines, or you could go for (M), which gives you 50 machines at $12 each. In that case you have a smaller Session amount but a load of machines to attack.

The breakdown you decide on is your own personal choice. You are neither right nor wrong in your decision.

So, with the $600 Bankroll, I'd go to the dollar machines with (F), (G), (H), or (I).

The 50¢ machines would get either (I) or (J) and the quarter machines would be (L), (M), or (N) for at least 40 pops of $15 each. I'd surely find at least 4 or 5 hot machines in those 40 chances.

Sessions are important to your battle plan. Be sure you set the amounts before you enter the casino, not wait till you get to the Slots and then decide to whip out your pad and pencil.

4

The Little Three

When it comes to gambling, we are all reduced to victims of our own greed and stupidity.

Manny S. Tite is as tight as a drum when it comes to money. His paperboy had to give him a notarized bill each week, because he thought the kid overcharged 11¢ on one of his monthly statements.

But while tightwad Manny S. Tite is so cautious with his money in the real world, he steps into a casino and immediately starts to act like a dork, throwing chips around as if they were useless pieces of plastic.

That's because he thinks that's the way you're supposed to act in a casino. What a dumb illogical assumption!

So before we proceed with our play at each Session, let's go over something very important to our day in the casino. It has to do with our approach, and it's called "The Little Three."

Several pages back I gave you "The Big Four." That is an absolute mandatory need for everyone who gambles.

Watt E. Cey just scratched his head and asked what I said. He was so preoccupied leafing through the book, looking for the key to the treasure, that he skipped right over the chapter on the Big 4.

So did a lot of you. Okay, if you didn't skip over the chapter, name the Big 4 right now—in their order.

Come on—name them!

That space above symbolizes the inside of Watt E. Cey's head. A blank. We're only a few chapters into the book and already this dork has forgotten the four main things he needs to gamble successfully.

How many of you also failed to name the Big 4 in their order? Tsk, tsk, tsk.

Okay, you've sneaked back through the pages and wormed your way out of a guilt trip by saying you'd go over it again later. Sure you would!

Anyhow, the second phase of things to remember is the Little 3.

(1) Theory
(2) Logic
(3) Trends

Theory

Theory is an opinion, and if you know everything about the subject you are teaching, then you have a valid Theory—if that Theory works. I have a Theory about gambling. It is very conservative and it works. The next chapter goes over this Theory.

Logic

Logic is an intelligent approach to, or analysis of a subject. It is illogical for man to think he can fly. For that reason we don't live in trees or dive off buildings. It's an illogical way to get to the ground. Oh, it's quicker, but the sudden stops tend to become a nuisance. Stairs or elevators are the logical way to reach our destination. A chapter will be devoted to Logic.

Trends

Don't discount Trends. This is gonna be a supercolossal part of your day. Finding and utilizing Trends is gonna be a determining factor in the success or failure of your day. A very important chapter on Trends is coming up.

That gives you the Big 4 and the Little 3 to concentrate on. Master all of those things and you're home free in the land of gambling.

5

Theory

I already told you what Theory is but remember this: Theory is never wrong. Naturally you gotta know your subject before you can express an opinion, or have a Theory, but any fool could have told you that much.

Since I don't know my right arm from my left ear when it comes to most subjects, I don't express an opinion about those things. Mostly because nobody gives a pig's ear what I gotta say anyhow.

But there are several things of which I am an expert at and capable of giving my Theory:

(A) How to correctly throw a big curve in fast-pitch softball.

(B) How to correctly define the difference between the curve I throw in softball and the curves you see on Sophia Loren.

(C) How to devour a dish of chocolate and vanilla ice cream.

(D) How to gamble correctly.

Since the first three of these ain't gonna interest many of you, I'll keep the Theories to myself. But the fourth one (D) may be of interest to you. Otherwise why are you reading this book?

Surely not to absorb my Theories on (B), although I've got some strong ideas about that subject—but that's another story!

For right now, accept the fact that my Theory on "How to Gamble" is effective. It ain't gonna make you rich but it ain't gonna break you.

My Theory has to do with minimizing losses. Wait for a hot Trend or machine and then use strong Money Management methods to take advantage of that streak. Simple but effective Theory.

It encompasses the art of knowing when to quit as a winner, regardless of the amount of the profit, or when to quit at a certain Loss Limit.

My Theory is very conservative. It is geared both to the high roller with a heavy Bankroll and the player with a small average Bankroll.

It is aimed at the philosophy of holding losses to the bare minimum and capitalizing on streaks as soon as they appear.

Maybe you won't like my Theory because it's so conservative. Okay, then come up with your own and I truly hope it works for you.

But before you go off half-cocked about "taking the shot" in the casino, at least look over my Theory. Maybe, just maybe, a few of the methods will cut some of your losses.

Have I got your attention?

Maybe. Maybe.

6

Logic

Anything to do with gambling has a logical explanation. Hitting a hard 15 in Blackjack is an illogical move when the dealer is showing a 5 as his up card.

There's no way he can turn over a card and beat you, so you know he has to take a hit. And the *only* time a dealer breaks in Blackjack is when he has to take a hit.

So let him do the hitting instead of your banging away with that lousy 15. That's a logical approach to a situation at a Blackjack table.

In the same view, if you had a hard 14 (ten, four) and the dealer showed a Queen as his up card, the logical move would be to hit that 14. If you stood on it, the dealer could expose his hole card—and if it's a 7, 8, 9, 10, Jack, Queen, King, or Ace, he would automatically beat you.

That's 8 ways out of 13 cards he would beat you, just by turning over a card. Of the remaining cards he could turn over (2, 3, 4, 5, 6), he would have to draw out. And one of the five times he would get seventeen through twenty-one and beat your lousy hard 14.

That makes 9 out of 13 times he'll beat you, so the Logical move would be to hit the 14, not because you got a good chance of winning, but because if you don't, you got a sure-pop 9–4 edge on losing.

Everything we do has a Logical approach or else it should be a Logical approach.

1) We put food in our mouth, not in our left ear.
2) We walk on our feet, not our hands.
3) We put gas in our car, otherwise it won't move.
4) Men zip their pants in front, not in the back.
5) We tell our wives how beautiful they are, otherwise they watch you like a hawk.
6) We tell our kids how tired we are, otherwise we'd have to help with their homework and they'd know how dumb we are.

All of these things are Logical approaches to situations that come up and we naturally handle it in a Logical manner.

I showed this list to my friend, Swift E. Knott. He agreed with all of my examples except for (4). I tried to explain it in Logical terms but Swift E. Knott is not too swifty.

Maybe some of you won't see the Logical part of gambling, where you are playing a game that offers you no better than a 50–50 chance of winning. How can you hope to double or triple your Bankroll?

Oh, you can hope, but how many times do you do it? If you said "Not too often," then maybe you haven't approached it from a Logical standpoint.

That's all I'm asking you to do. Look at gambling with a Logical, intelligent game plan.

Try to accept this Theory because it is Logical: A conservative approach of grinding out small returns. It beats losing anytime.

7

Trends

Bingo! This is what we're looking for: Trends in gambling! I don't give a horse's head if you refute a lot of my teachings but zero in on this one.

It is the ability to see when a Trend is happening and having the brains to take advantage of it.

Or it is the ability to see when you're in a losing Trend and have the brains to quit.

In gambling, Trends dominate, whether they be hot or cold. It's impossible to determine why or what makes these Trends so dominant; but rather than try to explain why they happen, 'cause I don't know, it's easier to get you to look for and recognize them while they are happening, not wait for the Trend to end and cry over the fact you missed that hot streak.

My friend Lee Tillate is a little slow on the draw. He never sees the forest until he bumps into a tree. His grasp of anything happening is always a day late.

Last week in the casinos he was playing at a BJ table while I was at Craps. When I walked up to his table he was gushing all over:

"Wow, can you believe it, the dealer just broke 23 times in a row."

I said, "Great, how much did you win?" He gave me that dumb look and even dumber reply: "Nothing, of course. I was

29

charting the table and wanted to see how long the cold spell would last—isn't that great: So I bought in and I've been playing for about an hour against her."

"So how're you doing?" I asked. "Oh, I'm out $600 'cause she turned hot, but it'll change again," he said.

I walked away, knowing Lee Tillate was very late getting into the game when the dealer was ice cold and later still getting out when the dealer turned hot.

He never took advantage of that cold streak by the dealer— and how many of you tell me the same old war stories about not cashing in on these Trends?

By the same token, when the table goes against you, why do you buck that streak?

Lee Tillate was late in getting in and later getting away from that game. These things happen at the tables, just as they do at slots.

You're gonna find Hot Slots and Cold Slots. That's called Trends. They occur many many times during the course of a day. Being able to take advantage of these Trends is what I'm gonna teach you.

But much much more important, is that you become aware of when you're in a Cold Trend and that you know when to leave a machine.

The most important part of the Little 3 is Trends. In fact, it probably should be clumped in with the Big 4.

But most of you have trouble remembering the Big 4. How could I possibly expect you to remember the Big 5!

Quick—name the Big 4! In order!

Isn't that a crime! 88% of you failed miserably. And you wonder why I question why you gamble.

8

Short Bankroll

I've alluded to this matter in past chapters but let's put it on the table and address the situation in a no-holds-barred manner.

Most people don't take the proper amount of money to the casinos 'cause they don't have it. Plain and simple, these people don't have money to gamble.

Sure, they still find a way to hold off paying a bill, or cutting down on dessert spending for a week, or collecting a few bucks at Birthday time to put together a little roll, but all in all, most people don't have the money to gamble.

They operate with what is called a Short Bankroll, and yes, this does restrict their play, 'cause it cuts into playing time and the chance to stay at a machine longer, waiting for a Trend to develop.

Many senior citizens are jeopardized by Short Bankrolls 'cause they're on fixed income, and rarely have the bread to compete.

So they try to make their coins last as long as they can, but then their Money Management methods suffer, because they begin playing by the clock, rather than taking advantage of the occasional streak that appears.

So if you are one of the many people who are forced to play "short," please don't let it affect your play. You are not wrong in not having the money, you're only wrong in not knowing how to control or manage that money.

My friend Les Kash has a smaller Bankroll than his gambling buddy Lotta Bredd, who has a never-ending flow of green.

But Les Kash knows how to manage the cash he has on hand and while his returns are not gigantic, his losses are never staggering.

He recognizes the fact that he has less cash to play with and is content with small consistent returns.

On the other hand, Lotta Bredd occasionally gets the big pay-day but more often plays like her money is a disease and she pours it into the machines in a nonstop frenzy.

When she does hit, back go the profits in a never-ending chase for the elusive jackpot. No Money Management.

I know a lot of you are playing short. So be it!

Just zero in on the methods coming up and you'll see your stake start to rise.

9

Scared Money

The sister to a Short Bankroll is a Scared Bankroll and most times they run hand in hand.

If you play short, you'll play scared and if you play scared you'll be afraid to pump up your bets when you start to win, 'cause you're scared you'll start to lose and since you have a short Bankroll to start with, you'll throw all Money Management out the window.

You see how one shortcoming affects your play and vice versa? Again, I'm not knocking you for playing scared, just warning you that if you do, it'll affect your chances of winning.

My friend Mae Shaker is a slots player who brings $40 to the casinos twice a week because she loves the action, the dream of hitting the jackpot and the chance to leave her problems at home and be surrounded by other people, all looking for that little extra zing in their day.

However, Mae Shaker may shake out of her dress, she gets so nervous. Why this reaction when things are going bad? Because she is caught in the "Scared Money Syndrome."

She feels that with 4–5–6 straight losing days she won't be able to return to her casino of dreams—and this leaves her all shook up.

She's not alone. There are people who actually get sick when they start to lose, or sweat, or get faint, develop a headache or a stomachache, or other symptoms that are all caused by the reaction of the Reality of losing money.

They have a right to feel this way because it's normal. None of us want to lose and those with Short Bankrolls feel it the worst.

Senior citizens and people down on their luck use the casinos and the Slots as a "beacon," or "dream place" where there is the possibility of good things happening, things that will change their lives.

My intent is not to close out that dream or smother the hope of winning money, but only to put it into perspective. I want you to realize what chances you have of winning and how to accept percentage returns.

You got a Short Bankroll or a Scared Bankroll, you don't got a problem—you got a situation that exists and which calls for you to accept and deal with.

Heck, I play scared every day. I'm petrified to call Racquel Welch on the phone, but I keep dreaming and someday, even with my Short chance of meeting her and Scared ability to try, I still keep dreaming.

So I don't want you to allow any shortfalls to disturb your play, only get you to accept the situation and then play within the amount you have to compete with.

Sure, I've said that before, but you weren't listening then and I doubt if I've even finally convinced you yet.

10

Proper Session Money

You've probably already forgotten the number 30, so try and associate it with something in your life that coincides with that number.

I find it very easy to remember the number 30, as all through my life it kept popping up:

a) In grammar school, the nuns kept me after school 30 days a month. (October, December, January, and March I got a day's reprieve.)

b) In high school, the average mark on my Algebra exam was 30.

c) 30 was the number of losses my basketball team averaged over a four-season span.

d) I was 30 when I discovered girls knew more about life than men.

e) 30 was the exact number of times Genevieve Plunk said no to my request for a date before I realized she wasn't kidding.

f) 30 was the number of days my wife gave me to leave the house after I told her I lost 28 straight days at the casino. (I lied, it was 30 straight.)

So you need these little associations to guide you in remembering the key numbers I give you to retain.

For now we'll take different sizes of Bankrolls, divide them into Session amounts and use those Session figures to determine what machine you may play at:

Your Slot Bankroll	# of Sessions	Session Amount
$ 100	Ten Play at 25¢ Machine	$10
$ 100	Twenty Play at 25¢ Machine	$ 5
$ 100	Five Play at 25¢ or 50¢ Machines	$20
$ 200	Ten Play at 25¢ or 50¢ Machines	$20
$ 200	Five Play at 25¢, 50¢, or $1 Machines	$40
$ 300	Thirty Play at 25¢ Machines	$10
$ 300	Ten Play at 25¢, 50¢, or $1 Machines	$30
$ 400	Twenty Play at 25¢ or 50¢ Machines	$20
$ 400	Ten Play at 25¢, 50¢, or $1 Machines	$40
$1,000	Twenty Play at 25¢, 50¢, or $1 Machines	$50

I think you get an idea of what I'm trying to do. It calls for you to take your Bankroll, whatever it may be, divide it into the number of Sessions you want to play at and make sure that the machine you play at does not exceed 30 times your starting Session amount.

This keeps you playing within the confines of your starting Slots Bankroll and keeps you away from the high-priced slots, until your Bankroll coincides with your desire to play at higher machines.

The next two chapters are probably the most important in the whole book. Do not proceed unless you have a clear head.

11

Win Goals

This and the next chapter are two of the most important messages you will receive in this book. Maybe a little edge toward the next chapter on Loss Limits, but this one is a close second.

It is the goal you must set, based on the amount of money you take to battle. It's called a Win Goal, not a Win Limit. It is merely the Logical predetermined amount of money you are aiming for.

Wanda Most is a frequent visitor to the casinos and she and I were discussing setting intelligent goals and Money Management Theories.

Wanda Most is a knockout and captivates both players and casino personnel alike with her good looks, witty personality, high style of play and lavish tipping practices.

We spent a lot of time discussing goals and betting techniques and playing strategies and I finally got up the nerve to ask her what I told her was a very important question.

"Wanda, when it comes to gambling, what is your win goal on any given day?"

Wanda Most didn't blink. "I wanna win the most I can and I ain't stopping till I got 8 Slot Machines ringing out jackpots."

Wanda Most is like most people in a casino and maybe you're included. You wanna win a bundle!

Now I come along and throw a cold blanket on that type of thinking. I want you to set a Win Goal of 60% on whatever amount you bring to the casinos.

That means if you get ahead $60 on a $100 Bankroll, your goal is reached and you will then rat-hole your starting $100 Bankroll and 50% of that $60 and play with the Excess.

It means that I am giving you another number, to go along with 30 for you to stockpile in your brain.

Thirty is the key for determining the amount of your Session money, whereby you must have 30 times the amount of your original bet to start at a machine.

Sixty is the percentage of that Session money that will key you locking away a profit and playing with the Excess or extra money.

Don't go trying to understand all of this at once, as the Win Goal moves will be covered in great detail in the Money Management section. Right now it is both important and mandatory that you set this Win Goal on both your overall Bankroll and each individual Session.

Suppose you take $10 to a machine. Then $6 is your Win Goal! Suppose you take $20 to a machine, then $12 is your Win Goal.

Each individual machine or Session becomes its own personal war. I want you to get in the habit of setting these Win Goals, 'cause even though they sound small, you'll see all of this come together as you move through these Theories.

Notice that not once did I say, or even hint, that you would leave the machine when you hit your Win Goal. You're not going to and I don't want you to.

But the Win Goal is set to give you a point to shoot at, where you then sock away the amount of your starting Session money plus one half of that Win Goal (for instance, $3 of the $6 profit) and now you play with the extra $3.

Admit it now... how many of you *always* set this Win Goal at each machine? Don't lie!

Okay, I see where 30% of you do set a Win Goal and I'm

proud of you. Now, how many of you sock away a profit? No hands, just as I thought.

The Win Goal is half of two things you absolutely *must* set when you start a Session. It's gonna be hard but it works. Just remember: It is NOT the end of that Session, just a preset goal, then you'll make some adjustments.

You ain't gonna realize it yet, but just zero in on these few things as soon as you start a Session:

1) Set a Win Goal of 60% of what you started with.

2) When you reach that Win Goal of 60%, divide it in half.

3) Rat-hole your Session Money.

4) Rat-hole one-half of that profit.

That's enough for now, you've reached your Win Goal and you're still at that same machine.

Next comes the sister move to the setting of the Win Goal.

12

Loss Limits

Don't skip this chapter and don't miss this message. It is probably the most important thing I will ask you to do upon entering a casino.

It is setting Loss Limits. That means putting a limit on the amount of money you will lose at every single solitary machine.

It is a stopgap move that cuts losses and minimizes your chances of getting whacked in a casino.

Sure, you're gonna have cold days, losing days, frustrating days, choppy days. That's all part of gambling. If you can't accept the fact that you will have losing days, then you're kidding yourself.

These losing days are gonna come and nobody can predict when or how often, but they'll come.

I'm the best player in the casino and I still lose anywhere from 30% to 35% of the time.

The key is that on these days I am losing, I minimize my losses by cutting back, leaving cold tables or cold machines and putting a limit on the amount of money I will lose at any Session.

Unlike the table games, the Loss Limit is exactly the same as the Win Goal—60%. That means you don't have to tax your mind with another number to remember. Sixty percent Win Goal, sixty percent Loss Limit.

Notice I use Goal when I set my Win amount, 'cause when I reach that goal it is not a stop or limit on my play. It is just a point when I rat-hote a profit and continue on with 50% of that 60% Win Goal.

Ah, but the Loss Limit is a flat-out stopping point. You cannot spend one single, solitary, lousy, extra quarter. The instant your Loss Limit has been reached, you're gone, baby—gone!

The 60% Loss wraps up the Session and the balance of your Session money is pocketed, never to be touched again that day.

Suppose you broke your $200 Bankroll into 20 Sessions of $10 each and lost 60% of that $10 (six dollars). You take the balance of that $10, which is $4, slip it away and don't touch it until you reach home.

Realistically I'm telling you that a $200 starting Bankroll will never exceed a total loss that day of $120, even if you lost all 20 Sessions.

Since the extra $4 from those 20 losing Sessions is all stuck away, you have $80 with which to start your next Bankroll.

It is *absolutely mandatory* that you do not exceed the preset Loss Limit of 60%, but that doesn't mean you can't reduce that Loss Limit to 50% or 40% or 30% or whatever figure you choose.

I'll go over this in more detail in the next chapter, but for right now, either make up your mind that you can accept Loss Limits and will set Win Goals or else everything else in this book will be merely information, with no rock upon which to allow it to perform.

You can build a beautiful home in a swamp and eventually the foundation will pull that gorgeous home right under.

I can give you powerful Money Management Systems to use, but unless you have the backbone to build a strong gambling foundation, those systems *won't* or *can't* carry you.

It starts with the Loss Limits, my friend. You got the guts to set 'em?

I rather doubt it.

13

Variations of Loss Limits

Now I'm gonna give you variations of the Loss Limits but don't take it as an opportunity to throw out these restrictions.

All I'm gonna do in this chapter is give you the right to alter the percentage of loss that you will incur, before wrapping up a Session.

The key number is 60% because that's the absolute maximum amount that you can lose before wrapping up a machine, so that *can't* be changed.

But some of you may want to accept a lesser percentage and I want you to know that that is completely acceptable. Suppose you'd like to set 50% or 40% Loss Limits on a Session, that's Okay, but only if you still follow the procedure of putting away that balance and never touching it again that day.

You see, the worst thing that happens to people is that they play down to their last coin and leave a machine totally broke and that sets a psychological blot in your mind that you "can't win."

If you took $6 to a machine and lost it all, you get that "wiped out" feeling because you lost everything.

But if you took $10 to a machine and lost $6, you'd still take $4 with you and at least it wasn't blowout city, although it was the same dollar loss amount.

And really, do you honestly believe that if you lose $5 at a machine, those last 4-5-6-7 quarters are gonna recoup those losses?

Don't be sil, you're at a cold machine and "'tis better to turn and run away and have money to play another day."

Right about now that Slot sage friend of mine, I. M. Madork is screaming about a story he heard 7-8 years ago. Says I. M. Madork: "My wife's cousin's mailman, who has a sister in Buffalo, has a butcher whose barber's wife has a lover. He was down to his last three quarters: he popped them into a machine and won the progressive jackpot for $3,000,000.

"So if it can happen to him, it can happen to anybody!"

Then I. M. Madork smiles that contented smirk, settles back, confident that if it happens to someone, it could happen for him.

I. M. Madork is a dork and anybody who buys that poppy-cock winds up chasing the elusive dream their whole life. Gambling is a job.

Playing Slots should he handled the same way, by grinding out small returns to get started.

So if you wanna reduce your Loss Limit to an amount lower than 60%, I'm proud of you. Make it anything you want, but stick to it.

I especially recommend lower Loss Limits to those of you who bring higher amounts to a machine.

If you bring $10 to a machine, then 60% or a $6 loss is in line.

But if you bring $50 to a machine, then cut your Loss Limit to maybe 40%.

That gives you $20 to crack that one-armed bandit and that's plenty of shots.

So the higher the Session amount, the lower the Loss Limit.

You ain't done listening to Loss Limits. There's gonna be other chapters on this in the Money Management and Discipline sections.

Knowledge of
the Game

1

Origin of Slots

In my first book on Slots I wrote a pretty good chapter outlining exactly how the early Slots worked. Some old-time casinos in downtown Vegas still have some of these old-time machines, so it is my duty to let you know how they work.

Later I'll show you how the computer addition to Slots has come into play.

Following is a thumbnail explanation of exactly how the Slots work:

What can I tell you? What key do I have for opening up that pesty machine and sending those thousands of silver dollars flowing into your pockets? There is no answer. There is no way to come up with a system to beat these bandits. And that's just what they are, bandits.

They sit there, all bright and shiny, with their left arm pointed to heaven, of all places, pleading with you to fill their stomachs with your silver dollars, quarters, anything. It is sooooo easy. So exciting. Place a coin into the slot, pull the handle, and pray in anticipation that this time those symbols will light up the jackpot. You missed. Well, maybe next time. Dreamer!

I will give you background information on the Slots, some figures on vigorish, and some Discipline factors. The rest is up to you. You want to play; go ahead, it's your money.

Slot machines reared their pretty heads in 1895 when Charles Fey, an enterprising young mechanic, invented the first machine. It was named the Liberty Bell. Fey not only invented it, but distributed his prizes to gambling houses who split the take on a 50-50 basis.

Fey did not use the fruits that are seen on today's machines. His invention carried card symbols, such as diamonds, hearts, spades, etc. These devices were instant successes, and naturally lured other enterprising "inventors." Herbert Mills, an arcade games manufacturer, improved on Fey's invention and the battle was on.

The first machines had three reels, but used only ten symbols on each reel, as opposed to today's bandits which contain twenty symbols per reel.

If you were to take off the back of a Slot Machine, besides the usual amount of wires, levers, and screws, you would see three reels which are activated when a coin is deposited and the arm is pulled down. These three reels spin for predetermined seconds, and then come to a stop in 1-2-3 order, showing three of the symbols in the window on the front of the machine.

Since each real contains 20 symbols, such as cherries, plums, bars, oranges, and let's find the possibility of one certain combination showing up. Merely multiply the symbols on each reel, such as $20 \times 20 \times 20$ which equals 8,000 possible combinations. If one particular machine had its jackpot based on three bars and there was only one bar on each reel, the chances of that combination showing up would be 7,999 to 1. That's because there are 7,999 ways to lose, as opposed to one way of winning.

Naturally, to find the correct chances of your hitting a jackpot, you would have to examine each reel to find out how many bars are on these reels, and then figure your percentage chances.

For instance, the first reel might have seven bars, the second five bars, and the third reel, one bar. You would work out your possible chances of having those bars all meet together and arrive at the percentage possibility of a jackpot. Multiply 7×5 equals 35, $\times$ 1 for a total of only 35 ways that the jackpot on that machine can be reached out of 8,000 possible total combinations. Would you call that a fruitless (excuse the pun) endeavor? Well, if it isn't fruitless, it sure is rough.

Of course, in the meantime, there are small payoffs, such as one cherry, two cherries, three oranges, three plums, etc. The payoffs are not jackpots, as the payoff is smaller returns, such as 3 coins, 14 coins, etc.

Understand this about the Slot Machines. They are programmed to return a certain amount of money based on their input. That amount might be 87%. That means, for every $100 that is poured into a machine, it is programmed to return $87. The $13 that it retains is the vig your are fighting.

The machines are set to return a certain number of coins when a combination shows. By multiplying all of the possible combinations and applying the number of coins that it will kick off, you will find out what that certain percentage is. Take a normal $1 silver dollar machine. If the vig is set for 7%, that means the house retains 93% for that particular slot. All of the payoff combinations, which might total 45, for example, have different payoffs, such as 500 coins, 250 coins, 50 coins, 18 coins; all the way down to 2 coins for 1 cherry. If you could tabulate all of the returns and apply it to the total intake, you get your percentage of vig. That doesn't mean, naturally, that if you put $1 into the slot, you get immediately a return of 87¢ on a Slot that has a 13% vig. The percentages are spread over thousands of plays, and not in any set pattern.

If the machine is set to return 6,800 coins out of all of their combinations as against a possible 8,000 inserted, that merely means that the house is keeping 15% of the 8,000 coins, or 1,200, and giving back 6,800, or 85%. The state decides on what that percentage will be, and the casinos must stay within those laws. Maybe one machine retains only 8%, and the one next to it retains 11%. In the overall slot section, the house does stay within the letter of the law.

In Las Vegas there are some machines that return 96% and 97% of their intake. The operator can still realize a handsome profit from these machines, and at the same time provide excellent advertising about his establishment. There is absolutely nothing that beats the hot word that a certain game can be beaten.

Since the days of Charlie Fey, the bandits have improved to the point that they offer various combinations of symbols, such as bars, triple bars, 7's, bells, and all types of figures to lure the superstitious player.

But the percentages remain the same, and the house always retains the edge. It's called the hammer, and it hits you over the head every time you pull that arm down. Isn't it funny... you probably don't even feel it.

2

Percentages in Slots

Again I'm gonna repeat a chapter from my first book on Slots and it's only to give you technical follow-up on how to figure your chances of winning or losing on the old 20-symbol, 3-reel machine.

Take a few seconds to glance over this info:

Let's get a little technical for awhile. To better illustrate what you are fighting at the machines, let's try and give you an idea as to how to figure the vigorish against you.

Suppose we wanted to find out exactly what our chances of winning were. That could only be done by examining each reel and counting every symbol that is shown. Since this can never happen, as the casinos do not have the time to allow each player to satisfy their whims, we can only guess at the number of symbols of one kind to be found on a single reel. For example, breakdowns may be as follows:

REEL 1	REEL 2	REEL 3
Plums 5	Plums 4	Plums 4
Cherries 3	Cherries 6	Anything
Oranges 4	Oranges 6	Oranges 4

CHERRIES: A payoff on the cherries would be figured by multiplying the three on the first reel, by the six on the second and any one of the twenty symbols on the third reel. This gives you 360 combinations. That means of the 8,000 combos, 360 could be this payoff, and, of course, the return is only about four coins. Go over every possible payout that is shown on the front end of the machine, and figure how many ways each could be made and the numbers of coins that are returned, such as 14 coins for 3 oranges, 18 coins for 3 plums and so on. If you put 8,000 straight coins into a certain Slot Machine and know exactly what each payoff for all the programmed wins would produce, you would see what your percentage of winning would be. You can be sure that the machine is not set to return more than 8,000 coins over a certain number of cycles.

Back to our explanation on the cherries. When the single cherry appears on the first reel, simply multiply the number of cherries on reel 1, times the fourteen times that the cherry does not appear on reel 2, times anything that will appear twenty times on reel 3, and you have $3 \times 14 \times 20$, or 840 combinations. If the payoff is 2 coins, that slot kicks out 1,680 total coins for that situation.

If it were plums, the table would read $5 \times 4 \times 4$, or 80 possible combinations. If the three plums were programmed to return 10 coins, there would be 800 coins in all returned when three plums appeared.

As I stated in the previous chapter, the 8,000 possible combinations may be broken down to return 6,800 coins based on these various possibilities. The house still retains a 15% profit margin or vig.

These machines are not "fixed" to eat up thousands of coins before the payoffs start occurring. But they are programmed to return only a percentage of the total number of combinations. For instance, one machine could conceivably kick off two jackpots in 20 pulls of the arm, and also return a sizable chunk of money on the lesser combinations, all in the space of twenty or thirty pulls. But who is to say when this will occur. That's why they call it gambling.

I'm not trying to confuse you with a bunch of mathematical

mumbo-jumbo, just attempting to make you aware of what the slots are about. I hear so many people at the Slots pouring in coins and moaning that the casinos have the machines fixed. Baloney. They're not fixed, and the casinos don't have to cheat. They are working on percentages, and it is those percentages, plus your lack of D-I-S-C-I-P-L-I-N-E that destroys you.

A final note on this chapter. Go get yourself 8,000 quarters to equal the number of possible combinations that could occur. Simply place a coin in the slot for 8,000 consecutive pulls. Each time there is a payoff, you put the winnings in your pocket, and continue to insert one of the starting 8,000 coins into the bandit.

When you are finished with the 8,000 starting coins, take out all of the payoffs that you stuck in your pocket. The amount of these payoffs, as applied to the starting bankroll, will give you the percentage that the machine is returning. This is not a foolproof system, as you could have repeat combinations occur both for and against the player, since the machine is set to show random combinations.

This will give you an idea of the vig you are facing, but nobody will go to all of this trouble, as most people want to try other Slots.

Look over these examples until you completely understand the functions of the one-armed bandit. It is not complicated, and as I've said all along, the logic of it stands out—or is it illogic?

3

Micro-Dots

I held off giving you this chapter, as it is the only technical one in the book, so don't worry about the fact that you never heard of a Micro-Dot before.

I'll explain it in layman's terms and even so, it is not a chapter meant to help you play, only to let you know how the new-fangled machines work.

In this world of technology, the computer has even worked its way into the body of the Slot Machine. This is how the new Slots operate.

There is a computer chip controlled by a method called R.N.G. which stands for Random Number Generator.

The first two words are self-explanatory. It means that numbers are spun off randomly (no specific pattern) by this computer chip.

The fact that these numbers are "generated" by the computer gives the technicians a nice easy formula called: R.N.G.

This Micro Processing Computer Chip is in operation continuously, whether the machine is played or not. It determines when the symbols will stop, by shooting out signals every fraction of a second.

These millions of signals keep right on working, even if you're just standing there and not feeding any coins in. The numbers activate the various symbols and these results are 100% random, hence the name R.N.G.

You know that the machines are not fixed, because the determining factor is that fraction of a second whereby you may hesitate putting a coin in and when you finally do, you happen to catch the Micro Dots activating a combination that kicks off a profit.

The difference that I can see in comparison to the old machines is that years ago you knew there were exactly 20 symbols per reel for three reels and the total combinations were derived by multiplying 20 × 20 for the first two reels equaling 400 and multiplying the 20 symbols on the third reel to reach 400 × 20: 8,000 total combinations.

The new machine has a lot more stops per reel, with cherries, bars, double bars, triple bars, plums, oranges, 7's and the killer—blanks.

Naturally there are more ways to lose with all the blanks, but more ways to win with extra combos. But there is no cheating and that's what I'm trying to convey.

Just understand that this is a process where the electrical signal tells the machine when to stop the reels, showing a variation of symbol combinations, but still staying "random."

Payoffs are explained on the face of each machine and that's why it's important that you read every single possible payoff and the needed amount of coins required to get such and such a payoff.

Okay, you have had your lesson in the technical side and the use of R.N.G.'s. It's really not hard to understand, but in all honesty I cannot give you the exact number of combinations anymore, due to the added blanks and symbols.

If you ever inherit a key to a Slot Machine and wanna figure out the total number of combinations, for instance on a 4 reel machine, just count the number of possible "stops" that could occur per roll. Maybe there are 40 "stops" which include blanks and symbols. Multiply the 40 × 40 which is 1,600, then 1,600 by the 40 "stops" on the third reel which equals 64,000. Then the 64,000 by 40 "stops" on the fourth reel. That's 2,560,000 possible combinations on a 4-reel 40 "stop" machine.

Were you listening?

And you still wanna play the Slots? Naturally, the combos are fewer with fewer reels and fewer "stops," but at least dwell on what I just said.

Nuff said!

4

Nonsense!

I just wanna squelch some of the stories that people tell me about what they heard the Casinos do to increase business.

(A) HOT SLOTS BY THE DOOR: This one has to do with the casino having the best slots by the front entrance, so the patrons get suckered into coming in. This may have been true in the late forties and early fifties when the casinos first blossomed in Vegas. People were afraid or timid about walking into these "dens of evil." So hot machines may have been put by the front door and shills used to get the people interested. I still hear the garbage about this play today. Nonsense, complete fallacy.

(B) HOT SLOTS ON CORNER: Same theory, different location. In this fairy tale, the hot machines are on the "outside rows" so you get hooked into playing more and more. Ever walk through the Slot section in a typical casino? There are over a thousand machines, and 627 reasons why this theory is dripping with baloney. There are 308 "outside rows."

(C) SLOT MACHINE SECRET BY MECHANIC: Continuing through fairyland, this one has the repairman as the only person who knows that a certain Slot Machine has been "doctored" to kick off a 110% profit. Sure, this guy goes to all the trouble to fix a machine, and then doesn't tell his family or friends! You swallow this story and you're eligible for the old "oil well in my backyard scheme." You call me and and for a lousy

$1,000 I'll sell you a piece of that oil well, 'cause I don't wanna get oil under my finger nails.

(D) SLOTS PAY OFF AT NIGHT: This one is the granddaddy of all fables in this Mother Goose tale. The casino fixes the machines to pay off only for the people who play at night.

Yeah, they make an announcement for everyone to leave the casino for 10 minutes and while everyone waits outside, they fix 1,500 machines to start paying off. This is done every day about 5 P.M.

For you people who buy this whack-job, I won't sell you a piece of an oil well. For you I have a movable Gold Mine. Just send me $1,000 in twenty-dollar bills and I'll send you an envelope of seeds that you plant anywhere you want on your property, and in three months you'll have your gold mine.

The scary thing is—I'll get a bushel of mail requesting this deal.

My friends, go back and look over these examples. If you believe or even heard of them, send 2¢ to the IRS. We'll pay off the National Budget in three weeks 'cause these stories have been around for decades and keep multiplying in infinite lunacy.

Knod N. Agree just woke up and heard me mention these stories. "Hey, that's right, I heard all these stories—they sound pretty logical to me."

Figures: this guy's dumber than Ken Knotspel. He couldn't spell "at" if you spotted him the 'a.'

5

Should I Play Dollar Slots?

You ain't got the right to make this decision. Your Bankroll decides, not your own gut desires or wants or needs. You got a heavy Bankroll, go for it. You got a short Bankroll, you cannot play dollar slots.

Sure I've told you before that the dollar machines **MAY** pay off at a higher return than the 25¢ machines, but that doesn't give you the right to break the rules of Bankroll to go for bigger game.

There's always the chance of losses in gambling and people with short Bankrolls, playing at high machines, tend to get whacked more often because their staying power is restricted by short money to play with.

Also, let's suppose you read the payoffs on a certain dollar Slot and find that the jackpot of 7 - 7 - 7 will kick off a $1,000 jackpot if three coins are deposited.

It may say that playing one dollar will only give you $100 if 7 - 7 - 7 shows. Naturally you're gonna wanna insert the called-for three coins. That's suicide for the low-heeled player and the fact that you **MAY** get a better return on the dollar Slots is not your green light to play them.

It takes all parts of the Big 4 to have a 50-50 chance of winning and I don't want you breaking even one rule.

I know you forgot how much money you need to play at a

machine, so for those with the short memories, the number is
30.

Thirty times your first bet. If that is $3, then you need $90
per machine. If you play 10 different machines, that's $900.

You got $900 with you? Then get back down to the 25¢
machines.

6

Who Plays the Slots?

Anybody who says they don't play the Slots is probably pulling your leg.

We've all had the urge to feed those money grabbing bandits and why not? It's so easy to pop a few coins in the slot, wait for the bells, and get our hopes raised as the first 3 reels spit out 7 - 7 - 7, and then what seems like an eternity, we pray for the fourth 7, and then die as a lousy purple plum puts a damper on our wild dreams of fame and fortune.

We've all gone through it and we've all thought about it. The Slots are the backbone of the casino and without them, the rooms would seem almost vacant.

My friend Will E. Ever is a constant knocker of people who play the Slots. He thinks they are a waste of time and absolutely impossible to win at. He's always picking on his wife, friends and even strangers who happen to be at a machine that he may be walking past.

If you asked Will E. Ever if he'd ever play the Slots you can hear him screaming eight rows away that he's too smart for a sucker bet like that.

One day he was playing Blackjack with me and was going through a pretty bad run. He said he was gonna take a trip to the john and slid off the stool.

About an hour passed and he still hadn't returned. I decided to go looking for him, 'cause Will will not let many minutes go by in a casino without getting into action.

I headed for the nearest men's room when I passed a group of people watching some guy going through all sorts of gyrations, as he poured his dollars into a progressive Slot Machine.

The machine was scorching and the more it paid off, the more this guy would yell and scream.

You don't have to be a rocket scientist to realize it was my buddy Will E. Ever. I waited awhile and then went back to my table.

Eventually Will wandered over and I asked him where he'd been the last couple of hours.

"Ah, I got hungry and went out to grab a bite. So I think I'll wrap up Blackjack for the day and wander around until you're done." Off he went and maybe even hoping to find another gold mine in the land of the bells.

But did you notice how he wouldn't even admit that he had succumbed to the lure of the Slots? Many people feel that way and we've all taken our shot.

I admit I've played Slots plenty of times and envisioned making a kill. I still play today but in a more controlled, conservative way which you'll see in the next section. But I play. Why lie about it?

Just for smiles, let me list the type of people that do play the Slots. See if you can find yourself in the list:

(a)	Men	(k)	Blue Collar People
(b)	Women	(l)	White Collar People
(c)	Fat People	(m)	Casino Personnel
(d)	Skinny People	(n)	Professional People
(e)	Young People	(o)	Clergy
(f)	Old People	(p)	High Rollers
(g)	Tall People	(q)	Daily Visitor
(h)	Short People	(r)	Occasional Visitor
(i)	Rich People	(s)	Smart People
(j)	Poor People	(t)	Dopes

(u)	Unmarried People	(x)	High School Grads
(v)	Married People	(y)	High School Dropouts
(v)	Single People	(z)	College Grads
(w)	Divorced People		

Did you find yourself in that group? Of course you did. We all play the Slots.

My contention is that if you play them, treat them just as you would any one of the table games.

That means a strong Money Management method and fabulous Discipline. I can't stop you from playing the Slots but I may reach some of you with the chance of getting you to adopt this control angle.

Who plays the Slots? Everybody. Well, almost everybody. Not Will E. Ever. He'll never stoop so low.

Well, it's time to head into another chapter, so let me get my good buddy Will E. Ever. I know just where to find him.

7

Warm Slots/Fixed Arms

I gotta address this nonsense 'cause I hear all types of stories about the fact that if you feel the front of a machine and it's warm, then the machine is ready to kick off a jackpot.

The thinking is that when the machine is hot, or when the coins coming out of the machine are hot, then the surplus of money has reached near the motor and since there is no place to continue to store the coins, then you're sure to be in line for a payoff.

Pure nonsense—absolutely garbage. I've already explained to you about the R.N.G. factor in today's Slots and the 87% and higher payoff of the older machines.

These random situations are strong enough to maintain a balanced payoff. So I don't want you putting any stock in the "warm machine Theory."

Finally we get to the end of the myths in Slot playing with the old "Stagger Handle Method."

In this antiquated nonsensical, absurdly ridiculous fable, whether you win or lose is predicated on how you pull the handle and how long you hold that pull.

Here are some of the thoughts:

(1) Pull the handle very very fast and let it snap back.
(2) Pull the handle veerrrry ssllllooowwwlllyy, and let it go back verrry ssllllooowwwlllyy.

(3) Pull fast, return slooooow.

(4) Pull sloooow, return fast.

(5) Use a herky-jerky stagger method of pulling in intervals, of one second apart.

(6) Pull the handle and hold it for a period of 3 - 4 - 5 - 10 seconds and then return it.

You've probably got a dozen or so more methods to use as gospel proof but put them on the back burner. Like I've said, those R.N.G.'s keep pouring out of that chip every fraction of a second and the manipulation of the Slot Machine arm has zero impact on the result.

Slots run in Trends, both hot and cold. Oh, have I said that before?

Well, not many of you were listening.

I've got one system though, that is absolutely sure to work, but you gotta do everything right.

(1) It only works on Tuesdays.

(2) It only works between 3-4 A.M.

(3) The casino has to have an "E" in its name.

(4) You must wear something purple, but no underwear.

(5) You balance yourself on one hand and insert the coin with your toes.

(6) Pull the handle very sssllllooowwwllly holding it for 10 seconds at each inch.

(7) When you reach as far as the handle goes, hold for 3 minutes and 8 seconds exactly.

(8) You then let the handle slide back vvveeerrryyy sssllllooooooowwwwwwwllllllyyyyy.

(9) Use your right leg to control the handle by placing it between the back of your knee and thigh.

(10) Works better on rainy days 'cause humidity loosens the reels.

I've given you this system for free and you can readily see it has more Logic going for it than these old stories.

After you've won three jackpots with it, send me $1,000 and I'll send you some more Gold Mine Seeds.

8

"He Got My Jackpot"

The story you hear most in the casino is the wailing of a slots player who has played a machine for two hours, finally gives up and walks away.

Before you go three feet away, somebody runs up, drops a few coins into the machine you were playing and bangs out a $250 return.

You start cursing the guy who invented the Slot Machine but you're so far off base you make Dimmy Dimwit look like a Rhodes Scholar.

I've already explained that the R.N.G. (Random Number Generator) is working even when no one is at a machine. It keeps spitting out formulas for symbols to appear and since the number of decisions that are ignited in a two-minute span could be in the thousands, you would **NOT** have gotten that payoff even if you had remained at the machine.

It is not based on the next pull of the handle, but in what symbols are being activated in that multifraction instant of a second.

Your mind and hands cannot operate quickly enough to complete the pattern of inserting a coin and pulling that handle, even if you knew it was gonna happen exactly at 8 minutes 23 seconds past 4 o'clock. You couldn't complete the transaction.

So the next time you leave a machine and someone sits down

and picks up a win, it was not necessarily gonna be your score. Let me give you the best analysis of how fast these R.N.G.'s work. You're sitting on your porch sipping a nice cool lemonade, when all of a sudden Miss America, Miss World and Miss Universe appear on the top step. Before your dirty mind can even think of what your first thought is or before you can even think to think what it might be, a thousand R.N.G.'s would have processed 50 decisions on a typical Slot Machine.

This example is given to show you how fast the R.N.G. is. As much as I realize this fact, I can't believe our dirty minds are that slow—but that's another story.

Just accept this one—Slots decisions are one billion percent random. Period!

9

Why Do You Gamble?

This is the eighth book I've written and in each one I ask this same question: "Why do you gamble?" Veterans of my teachings know the answer, but do you?

Do you really know why you gamble? It's a four-letter word that drives you to risk money on the outcome of dice games, sporting events, card games, Slots or any such endeavor which calls for the risking of money to better your financial position.

Have you come up with that four-letter word? It's called NEED. Each one of us has a particular need that stirs our juices and makes us chase that elusive dream.

Look at this list and see if you can find yourself in one of these categories:

(A) Need Money
(B) Need Entertainment
(C) Need Outlet for Life-Style
(D) Need Thrill of Going for the Chase
(E) Need Feeling of Adventure

Surely you can find yourself on that list. I probably qualify for every one of them but especially (A). I gamble for money and am not ashamed to admit it.

Sure I love the excitement, the thrills, the chase, and I hate the losses that occur 30% to 40% of the time, and each loss hurts a lot.

But my need is making a living in the world I love, and it disgusts me to see people coming into my world and getting their clocks cleaned.

Some of you might have said GREED was what drew you to gambling (even though I qualified the question by saying it had four letters, not five).

But greed doesn't drive you to gambling. Greed takes over after the NEED is satisfied.

My friend Les Trubble has more trouble than a deep sea diver with a punctured lifeline.

He makes a decent living as a truck driver, but has run into some financial problems with two kids heading into college, his wife having an unfortunate hospital stay, and two cars that pick the same week to decide to drop a transmission.

Les Trubble accepted his troubles for awhile, but then started looking for ways to supplement his income and get out of trouble.

He read where some guy bangs a Slot Machine for $700,000 in just a few trips to the casinos and envisions his problems coming to an end!

Les Trubble thinks this can happen to him, so he starts dipping into his budget of mortgage payments and heads for the land of dreams.

In the short space of two hours, he finds a couple of generous machines and runs up a decent profit of $215. His spirits are soaring, his prayers answered.

On the way to the casino he told himself that even a $150 profit would cover a telephone bill, a dental visit and an insurance payment.

As soon as he reached this profit, with a couple of dollars to spare, his NEED was satisfied. But Les Trubble decided that this was his day and no use quitting while he's on a hot roll.

So armed with his starting Bankroll of $300, his profit of $215, his hot streak in third gear and his hopes soaring, he goes for the kill.

It's no contest. A cold run develops and he increases his bets.

Then some near misses frustrate him and he promises to quit if he just gets back to the plus point of $215.

But Lady Luck has flown the coop. The more he loses, the higher he bets. In a blink the profit is gone. In two blinks his $300 Bankroll is gone. Now Les Trubble has more trouble. He has to find a way to replace the stake.

The ride home is a nightmare. Not only is his money gone but his common sense. You know what this dork is thinking about? A way to get back to the machines 'cause he's gotta get that money back.

We've all traveled that road. I sure have. It's a lousy feeling, a lousy bottomless, gut wrenching experience.

And I see and talk to these people every day of the week. Different faces, different casinos, different games, same stories!

Why do you gamble?

10

Slot Charting

We've already alluded to the fact that charting a Slot Machine is different from a table game for several reasons:
(1) The R.N.G. (Random Number Generator) factor.
(2) Cold Slots are idle because they are cold.
(3) Hot machines are being used because they are hot, so you can't chart.
(4) In Craps, at a hot table, you can squeeze in and get involved with that streak.
(5) In Roulette, if your predetermined numbers are showing, you can jump in.
(6) In Blackjack, if the dealer is breaking, you can grab a stool and play against him.
Notice that charting the table games give you a chance to get involved in that game, even though other people are playing.

Not so with Slots, 'cause only one can play a machine. So we can't apply the same tactics. But at the same time we can't throw out this Theory of charting, looking to catch good runs.

There is a way around this problem and it incorporates heavier emphasis on two of the things I've been throwing out to you.
(1) Loss Limits
(2) Naked Pulls
With the added leaning on these two restrictions, it means

our Charting comes **after** we start on a machine and not before.

In other words, when we take a Session amount to the machine, say $10, we have no way of knowing what the previous decisions were, so our decision to stay at that particular Slot will be made after we start playing.

In simple terms, that means our guidelines will be set with the intent of leaving that machine as soon as we see that things are not going well for us. Hence the setting up of guidelines that I already imposed a few paragraphs back, but which you have probably already forgotten.

You know I have a friend, her name is Rhea Repeet, who has a great deal of trouble remembering the things I show her. So I have to repeat and repeat a lot of things, so Rhea Repeet grasps them.

A lot of you fall into that category, so that's why I repeat things. Especially the important things.

This is one of the important items, so for the benefit of Rhea Repeet and some others out there, I'll repeat this move:

(1) Set Loss Limit

(2) Set Naked Pulls

You already have had Loss Limits banged into you constantly, so you should by now realize that it is the percentage of your Session amount that is set, to limit your dollar loss.

That means you put a limit on the amount you can lose. I gave you 60% as the ultimate max, but you can drop it to 50%, 40% or even 30%. The lower you set as your Loss Limit, the less money you're gonna lose.

That last sentence was a mouthful. Read it 47 times. I'm sure even my friend Lee Tilhope, who has little hope of grasping my conservative Theories, can understand that message.

Naturally we'll be going back to Loss Limits, but it's the second restriction that I wanna elaborate on, and that'll be the crux of the next chapter.

So realize the importance of Charting and then swing over to my Theory of charting *after* the start of a Session, not before.

11

Rehashing Naked Pulls

You should all understand the meaning of the three words I use to describe this chapter.

Rehashing is simply going back over a method, giving you options to use for that move, but pinpointing exactly what the purpose of that exercise is.

All of you dirty-minded guys out there understand the word *naked,* but in this instance, it has nothing to do with your preconceived ideas.

There is another side to the meaning *naked* and it has to do with the word *empty.* Think of something that coincides with empty or nothing or zero.

A good example would be the empty head of Imus Pressit, a lousy non-disciplined casino player, who has an empty head when it comes to Money Management. Imus Pressit presses or increases every single solitary win he gets, never pulling back a profit.

He loses 90% of the time, 'cause he has zero Theory as to how to bet. He has an empty head, a zero reading on Theory of play. To put it bluntly: a naked brain when it comes to gambling. "There ain't nothing there."

So carry that last sentence forward: "There ain't nothing there."

If you are pulling a Slot handle and nothing is coming out,

they are called Naked Pulls. Nothing is happening. There ain't no Trend there and there ain't no profit there.

You wanna leave that machine when it's going cold. So you set a limit on the amount of zero results or empty decisions, or to be precise, Naked Pulls!

My friend Phil Theemind has a filthy mind and he is disappointed with my analogy or use of the word *naked*. But he should be the first to understand that naked is nothing, because that is what fills Phil's head, Zero Logic.

So I want you to set Naked Pulls where nothing happens. Even with the R.N.G. factor, you will see that Trends do develop. It isn't something that's easy to understand in gambling, but these Trends have a way of occurring: both good and bad!

Pick a number between 7 and 14. That will be your Naked Pull designated stop sign. Suppose you set 9 as your choice.

If 9 consecutive pulls result in zero returns, leave that machine. You're gonna say 9 ain't enough. Ask some poor woman with 9 kids if that ain't enough. Or have 9 straight days with a headache, or 9 straight hang-ups by your favorite lady.

How about 9 pops on the arm by a pest at your place of business, or 9 straight losing days at the track?

You gotta put a number out there somewhere, that keys your doing something about a bad situation. You have to realize that the "due to happen" is a lousy system, with nothing to protect you.

The Naked Pull Theory puts an end to a bad run. As I explained in the chapters on the R.N.G. factor, even if you leave that machine, it keeps spitting out activating numbers. So even if you go three steps and someone pops up to that machine and hits, you wouldn't have got it anyway and I know that is one of the reasons you hesitate to leave the machine.

Think about the Theory. Then think about a number. If you are a conservative player, you'll accept a low Naked Pull number. If you are aggressive, you'll try to stretch the Theory, which means you've broken it, and there ain't no room for error in my conservative approach.

If you can't or won't accept a max of 14 straight Naked Pulls, you're gonna have a lot of trouble later on in this book where I really zero in on Discipline.

I even think my dirty-minded friend Phil Theemind is starting to waver. That's a plus, getting the empty-headed ones to comply. Come on, give it a try!

12

Wrapping Up Knowledge

We come to the end of the second part of the Big 4: Knowledge of the Game. However, in Slots, the amount of Knowledge is not really 25% of the Big 4, since this is not essentially a game that requires moves and strategies.

But the Knowledge that was covered in this section is aimed at making you aware of many of the things needed to gamble sensibly.

In the Bankroll section there were mandatory chapters that demand to be re-read, such as Win Goals and Loss Limits.

This section has a lot of information essential to your playing the slots, but only a few of the chapters call for a positive review:

1) Micro-Dot explanation of the R.N.G. factor.
2) Reading the Glass
3) Reality (Read it six times)
4) Slot Charting
5) Naked Pulls

These are five of the chapters that contain messages that give you a Knowledge of the things that are a part of the whole package.

Look at #3, Reality. That is a super-important part of your grasp on gambling. You've got to become aware of the dangers that gambling presents when you start losing.

A lot of people lose control and do things they would never do in their real life roles or jobs.

My friend Stu Pitt is a very smart person; in fact, he borders on genius. He has taken several companies and by strict Money Management and intelligent business decisions, turned them into empires.

In the business world he is recognized as a giant among men.

Stu Pitt loves the casinos, plays a lot of Craps and Blackjack and is well known by the casino personnel. In fact, he is known as a giant dork.

His illogical play, crazy betting habits, and lack of discipline has earned him the title "Stu Pitt: the pits of stupidity in the crap pit!"

Now, what turns an intelligent guy in the real world into a dork in the land of gambling? I'll tell you what it is:

a) A lack of Reality about what gambling is all about.

b) An illogical assumption that gambling is a snap to win at.

c) A self-planted illusion that gambling will make you rich.

Stu Pitt is not the only stupid person in the world of gambling. A lot of us fall prey to those three examples and it all revolves around the lack of the Big 4.

This section was to make you aware of the things you need to gamble sensibly. Tied in with the important section on Bankroll, it was really just a warm-up for the meat of your play. That's called Money Management.

So before you slide into that section, be sure you've gobbled up and digested the pertinent information laid out so far.

I'll be alluding back to these chapters over and over, so you better be aware of what was said.

Imus Pressit just asked Stu Pitt what R.N.G. was. Stu Pitt, in complete annoyance replied: "Weren't you paying attention, you jerk. He was telling us that slots is a R.N.G.: Real Nice Game."

And you wonder why they build stalls for donkeys!

Money Management

1

Do You Want Money Management?

Nah, not really. Because if you really wanted it, you'd have a controlled style of play by now. Most of you reading this book fall into one of the following categories:

a) **Frustrated Player:** Goes to the casino with $200, gets ahead, has nothing to do, gives back profit and returns home mad, frustrated and disgusted.

b) **Desperate Player:** Has $100 to invest in gambling. Needs money so badly, constantly plays progressive machines in hopes of getting the kill. Thinks this book will give you location of next machine to spin off jackpot.

c) **Curious Player:** Deep in the back of your mind you believe there's a method of betting sensibly. Reads all types of literature on gambling but when finally gets to the casino, plays with a "What the heck, let it all hang out" attitude.

d) **Cynical Player:** Gets book to learn how to win, but laughs and smirks at the suggestions to break Bankroll into Sessions, use Money Management, and quit with small profit. Swears that only chickens and gutless players accept small returns.

e) **Sharp Player:** (There are only two of you.) Realizes that gambling only gives you a 50-50 shot and wants some type of game plan to follow. Is receptive to suggestions.

f) **The Dork:** Has lost 87 consecutive trips to the casino. Swears to follow every Discipline plan and does. Gets ahead $225 and heads for the door. Three machines from daylight tells self, "Just one more Session." Finally reaches car, after having blown back the $225 profit, plus the $200 he brought, plus the $200 from his credit card, plus $50 he borrowed from his wife, plus two quarters he found on the floor, plus $3.50 he got selling his shoes to a passerby.

Somewhere in that list you will find yourself. You've heard of Money Management, but think it's only in the minds of fools. You say you want it, but when push comes to shove you'd push me away and tell me to shove my suggestions.

Next time you're in a casino, just head over to the slots section and zero in on a couple of machines.

Watch the erratic betting habits of some players, basing their play strictly on the gut feeling they have at that particular instant.

Watch some guy get ahead at a machine and then re-deposit every single solitary coin back in... even if it is 123 consecutive losing pulls.

Sure, you say you want Money Management but only two out of every hundred of you will do the things I demand you to do. Two out of one hundred!

2

Minimizing Losses

Don't skip this chapter. This is for all people who gamble, who think about gambling, who've heard of gambling, who knows someone who gambles, or in any way shape or form engages in the process of risking money for a return.

This in a nutshell encompasses my whole Theory and will forever change your approach to gambling.

It is the art of minimizing losses that will determine your future in this very nasty business.

I'm gonna give you a quote to remember, but of course just like my friend Ivor Gott, you too will forget it in just a few more chapters.

"It ain't how much you win at gambling that is important, it's how little you lose."

You look at that statement, memorize it, follow it, and you'll be a successful player.

You've heard me allude over and over how so many of you look at gambling as your savior, your way out of the doldrums, your path to untold riches. That's because most people look at gambling as only an avenue to big fortunes.

But if you don't have the bread to bet, you can't compete and I've already pointed that out in the Bankroll section.

Now I want you to concentrate on holding your losses down, by realizing that Loss Limits are your big keys to control.

There are high rollers like Igott Bredd who don't have to worry about their Bankroll and they can last a long time. Long enough to be able to capitalize on a streak. That's why you hear of big kills in the casino. It's done by people with big Bankrolls.

The average Bankroll for a person in the casino is $300. That means if you lumped every single player who walked through that door, including the high rollers with $5,000 to play with, you'd come up with an average of $300.

That ain't a lot of money for a day in the casino, especially if you seriously adhere to my Loss Limit philosophy, that restricts you to an absolute ceiling of 60% of what you bring.

A lot of you bring $100 and that's a lot of money to lose, whether you wanna believe that or not.

So I come along and say: "Okay, what I want you to do is hold down your losses, so you don't get wiped out."

In a blink, Imus Pressit, who presses every single winning bet he ever had, is organizing a lynch mob to shut me up. He claims I am depriving you of the fun of going for the big bundle.

No, I ain't. What I am trying to get you to realize is that on the days that things are going bad, hold your losses down and bring back some of your starting Bankroll.

If you can't win anything with the first 60%, there's no guarantee the next 40% will do it for you.

And since you're in a cold run, there's the chance you could slip further into the slide toward wipeout. That hurts and you know it. You've gone through it and so have I.

So zero in on this message. Minimize your losses. As my old pappy used to say: "'Tis better to turn and run away, with money to bet another day."

Ivor Gott, who already forgot, asked me to repeat the earlier message.

"It ain't how much you win at gambling that is important, it's how little you lose."

Memorize it!

3

You Wanna Win Big?

This is for all you people who up to now have scoffed at my suggestion (demand—if you wanna know the truth) to go for consistent small returns.

These people, led by their aggressive leader Wanda Johnpott, want only to win the jackpot. They don't wanna accept 20% or 30% or even 50% returns. Wanda and her crew want big bucks.

Okay, let me show you how to win a lot of money in the casino. Bring a lotta money to the casino. You wanna win big? Bet big.

Other than being at a scorching machine when that R.N.G. finally bangs out the right combination, the only way you're gonna win big is to bet big. And if you don't got a big Bankroll, how can you expect to bet big?

It's a vicious circle that leads you on a merry-go-round of frustration, but that's the way the wig wags.

Let me give you an idea of Logic, as applied to gambling. Let's suppose you took $100 to the casino and I asked you if it was easy to win $3.

You smirk and crow: "Of course it's easy to win $3 with $100. Who can't get $3 ahead?"

I ask people if they'd accept $3 as their profit for the day, since it came so easy. Again the smirk and the quick retort!

"Are you crazy? Why would I go all the way to the casinos for

81

a lousy $3, no matter how easy it was to make it?"

Of course the conversation is tilted toward the player so far, 'cause it **IS** easy to win $3 with $100 (lousy $3 if I wanna get my quotes right).

Okay, if it's so easy to win $3 with $100, then why not bring $1,000 to win $30, or even $10,000 to win $300. It's the same percentage, the exact same percentage. And I guess you could struggle along on $300 a day, since by your own admission, you find it so easy to win 3% of your starting Bankroll.

Oh, you don't have the $10,000? Then how about $5,000 and accepting the same 3%, then maybe you could raise it a notch to 5%, which is a $5 return for your $100. Most of you started with $100, but you won't quit. It's too small for your expensive desires.

Yet it is the exact percentage of winning $500 with $10,000 and even that aggressive boyfriend of Wanda Johnpott, Dewey Druel, is doing a lot of drooling over the possibility of winning $500 a day.

But even though the percentage is exactly the same, people like Wanda and Dewey can't grasp the Logic of accepting percentage returns.

Okay, you don't have $10,000 to gamble or $5,000, or even $1,000. I understand that. But a 5% return on $1,000 is a tidy $50 kickoff per day, based only on the fact that it is exactly like $5 on $100.

So if you don't have the proper Bankroll to give you this so-called easy 5% return, then why not wait until you are properly qualified?

Why keep blowing $100 here and $200 there, going for the dream, when you could save up for a decent Bankroll and accept that 3% or 5% return?

Now, if you said it's NOT easy to win $3 on $100, then why are you betting in the first place?

If it's hard to win $3 on $100, then it's gotta be downright impossible to win $1,000 with $100.

Wanda Johnpott wants the jackpot badly, but now she is

starting to wonder if maybe this example is a Logical approach. At least she's thinking.

Her dorky boyfriend, Dewey Druel, still drools at the thought of the mega-buck payoff.

He spits all over his chin as he proclaims:

"Yeah, but at least some day I might win the big one and people who only go for small returns will never know what it's like to win big."

People like Dewey never know what the meaning of WIN really is. They spend their life chasing the carrot.

And end up going in circles.

4

Entering the Casino

If you're still with me, let's go back and lay out your day so far. This will bring you right up to the casino doors, with all of the things laid out for you, based on your own personal Bankroll.

Note that this does NOT include the way you will play that day, just pre-sets the important part of your preparation.

As you have already read, these things will be predetermined.

1) Set aside your Bankroll,
2) Decide on game you will play (Table or Slots),
3) Divide your money into Sessions,
4) Predetermine your Win Goal,
5) Predetermine your Loss Limits,
6) Set Naked Pulls,
7) Make sure you predetermined your Loss Limit,
8) Based on your Session money, decide whether you will play 25¢, 50¢, or $1 slots.

NOTE: This is a decision that your Bankroll will make. For every single person who takes less than $300, you are a 25¢ or 50¢ player. For every person who takes $100 or less, you are a 25¢ player. It is the people with Bankrolls higher than $300 that I am giving the choice to.

Go back over that previous paragraph until you know, understand, and agree to follow.

My friend I. M. Madork will be dumb enough to con himself into taking $100 total Bankroll and going to the dollar slots. If you have the mind-set of a dork like I. M. Madork, then you're just kidding yourself.

At least when you go broke quickly, playing dollar slots with a short Bankroll, you'll have someone to sit and talk with, while you wait for your bus to take you back home. I. M. Madork spends a lot of time sitting and talking.

Setting Aside Your Bankroll

Don't break one single rule.

If it's $200 or $2,000, it is your stake and every single solitary move that day, from the type of machine to the Win Goals, to the Naked Pulls, is based on that Bankroll. It determines your Session amount and your whole betting process.

You wanna win big, bring a big Bankroll. You don't got a big Bankroll? Then accept what you got and make your moves with what you got.

Deciding On a Game

Since we're talking Slots in this book, I'm only interested in what you allocate for Slots. If $300 was your total Bankroll and you set aside $100 for Slots, then all your decisions on Slots are based on $100, not $300. The $100 will be divided into Slot Sessions and you are a quarter player.

Next chapter we pick up on Sessions, so before you go on, browse back through this chapter and lay out your money. That's your Bankroll. Now you divide that Bankroll into Sessions!

(Continued next chapter.)

5

Straight 60: System #1

I like this system. I like the Theory behind it. I like the tremendous number of spin-offs. I like the control factor. I like the results I've had with it.

It's snap city to grasp, because the explanation is right in the title. It's called the Straight 60 because the Win Goal is 60% and the Loss Limit is 60%. How much easier is it to grasp?

Suppose you walk up to a machine with $10 as your Session amount. You have a built-in Win Goal of 60%, which means you play until you win 60%, or in the case of a ten-dollar Session amount, six dollars.

That doesn't mean you leave the machine when you hit a profit of six dollars, but it does give you a goal to shoot for.

The next chapter tells you what to do with that six dollars, but just keep that figure in mind. You wanna win 60% of what you started with. With a $10 Session amount, setting a 60% Win Goal is a decent percentage.

On the same wavelength, you now set 60% as your Loss Limit. If you lose 60% of your Session money, you wrap it up, stick the remaining Session money in your pocket and walk.

With a ten-dollar Session amount, $6 is the absolute maximum amount of your possible loss. The remaining four dollars is rat-holed and can **NOT** be touched again that day.

Naturally you can't surpass the 60% Loss Limit, but you do

have the option of quitting before you hit 60%. Let's assume you're at a choppy machine that never kicks off your Naked Pull number, but it is not showing any positive streaks.

You keep losing 3 pulls, winning 1, losing 5, winning 1, losing 4, winning 2, losing 4, winning 1. Little by little you're eating into that Session amount but not reaching the Naked Pulls. You've lost 35% of your Session amount, nowhere near the 60% mark but you're going nowhere.

Why stay at that machine? There are thousands of machines around that you can take a shot at and some of them have to be better than the one that's grinding you out.

So even though you've got a Loss Limit of 60% with the Straight 60 System, you do have the option of walking before you reach that Limit.

The amount that is rat-holed in your pocket is 40% of what you started with. Let's say you started with $20 as your Session amount and caught a choppy Trend. Your Loss Limit is 60% of twenty dollars or $12. But you soon decide you wanna wrap up this machine after you get behind $8.

You leave the machine with an $8 loss and put 40% of the twenty dollars away, which is $8. The other $4 can be set aside to start another Session, along with any like amount of money from another earlier Session.

But you **MUST** bury 40% of the twenty dollars ($8) in your pocket and never touch it again that day.

It assures you of never going home broke, 'cause you'll always salvage 40% of every Session amount. I already told you that this was a psychological move so don't go saying you'll take $12 to the machine and lose it all 'cause it's the same as 60% of $20.

Baloney, you're losing every dime of a Session amount and eventually that wears on your nerves. Do what I demand! Take a Session amount, set a percentage of Win and Loss and learn Discipline.

The Straight 60 System can keep you at a machine a long time. You just keep replaying the coins over and over, hoping you catch a Trend, hoping you hit your Win Goal before your

Loss Limit.

Try this System. There'll be more on it a few chapters further on, but grasp the Theory.

Next comes a must-read chapter, a message that will constitute a gigantic input into your gambling.

Don't read the chapter until you have a clear mind.

Notice that this first System **DID NOT** show you any method of betting. This is the Money Management control whereby you play your System or any that I have coming up, but you adhere to the Win Goal of 60% and the Loss Limit of 60%.

You pick the System, I gave you the controls.

6

Guarantee and Excess

I finished the last chapter by telling you that this was a massive input into your Money Management approach and that I wanted you to have a clear head before you attempted to grasp the message.

Lo and behold, my friend Claire Hedd pops out of the woodwork. She approaches gambling with a muddled mind and no Logical method of play. If anyone does not have a clear head when it comes to gambling, it's Claire Hedd.

So for all of you reading this chapter, shake your head a few times to clear the cobwebs. Not you, Claire Hedd. I'm afraid if you shake your head, it'll fall off.

But the rest of you will soon see why this is an important part of your day. Again, the title of the chapter is the dead giveaway.

It is the move you make as soon as you hit your Win Goal.

1). You'll set aside a Guaranteed profit.

2) You'll play with the Excess.

Already you can see what a powerful approach this is. Let's go back to a Session amount of $10.

You take the $10 in quarters to the machine, plus two cups. One cup is empty, the other one has the ten dollars in it.

You play with the ten dollars until you either win $6 or lose $6. You already understand this. If you lose 60%, or in this case $6, you leave the machine. You already understand this.

What you really wanna know is, "What happens when I win $6, do I leave with the profit?" The answer is a resounding **NO**. You never leave a machine or a game when you're winning, or in a hot streak.

That doesn't mean you give the profit back to the house, but you do come up with a move that lets you do both:

1) Continue to play at that hot machine.

2) Eventually leave with a profit.

3) Make a move that wraps up that profit.

Which brings us to the title of this chapter and the move that will revolutionize your gambling.

It's called Guarantee and Excess and requires two moves. That's one more than my friend I. M. Madork is capable of doing at the same time.

Once I asked him to chew a piece of gum and blink at the same time. He couldn't concentrate on either one and ended up wetting his pants.

So I want you to concentrate real hard on the two simple little things I'm gonna give you:

a) Take the $6 you're ahead, which is your Win Goal, and break it in half.

b) One half goes in the cup that was empty and this is called your Excess.

c) One half goes in the cup which has the $10 Session money. This is called your Guarantee.

That's it, breaking the $6 in half will take two seconds (two and a half hours for you cats who are a little slow in arithmetic).

The second move takes about ten seconds, placing one half of the coins in the empty cup and putting the other half in the cup with the Session amount.

Look what you've done. You've got your starting ten dollars Session amount in a cup and you've added 50% of the $6 Win Goal, which is a locked-up profit of $3. You're guaranteed to leave that machine with at least a profit of one half of what you got ahead.

We're not done yet, but I hope you see the power of this

move. Most people who get ahead at a machine never know when to quit.

They keep playing and eventually pour the profits back. Handling the Win Goal with this approach is a supercolossal move which doesn't take much brains, but does take a lot of guts.

Go back over this chapter until you grasp the Theory. Then we move on to the next step.

7

Handling the Excess

Here is the second part of your big move when you reach your Win Goal. It concerns your Excess, the other half of that Win Goal, where you got ahead at a certain machine.

Sure, you're gonna get ahead many times, but it's the sharp people who know what to do when they get ahead. Anybody can take that profit and pour it back into the machines. That takes no brains.

But the smart person who gets ahead at a machine has accomplished what he or she set out to do; that is, get ahead.

Here is where I step in and take control of your next move. The past couple of chapters showed where you break that money in half, setting aside your starting Session money and one half of that profit. Now you got a Guaranteed win all salted away. You're still at that machine with the other half of that Win Goal, which is called your Excess.

You can continue using the same method that got you to this point or you can get a little aggressive. For now I'll keep you at the conservative level. A little deeper into this section we'll go over a move called Plateaus, but just hold your britches.

You gotta feel good at this point. Your Session money is safe, a profit is locked up, and you're at a productive machine. The only other thing you guys could hope for would be to have Loni Anderson slide into the next seat, but that's another story.

Some of you won't like this next move, but before you condemn it, think about the Logic of it. You're playing with one half of your Win Goal which is called your Excess. Every subsequent payoff has to give you a guaranteed profit. Let's say your next pull kicks off two Cherries for a three-coin return. Put one coin with your Guarantee, two coins with the Excess.

Next three pulls have no return but then comes three bars and a ten-coin payoff. Pay yourself 5-4-3-2 or 1 coin. Just grab the amount of coins you predetermined to rat-hole and place them with the Guarantee.

Notice how every subsequent win at that machine, after the Win Goal has been reached, results in a payoff to your profits. You keep increasing your Guarantee and at the same time increasing your Excess.

You're still controlled by your Loss Limit and Naked Pulls, but now you've zeroed in on milking that machine for as many coins as you can.

As long as you keep winning, you stay at that machine but keep paying yourself. The amount of coins you set aside with these Excess wins is immaterial. You do whatever you feel comfortable with, starting with putting aside one coin, up to one half of the win.

I have guides that I use. Maybe you'll like these or maybe you'll wanna set your own. The amount you set aside goes with the Guarantee. The balance stays with the Excess:

Profit	Set Aside
1) 3 coin win	1
2) 4 coin win	2
3) 5 coin win	2
4) 8 coin win	4
5) 10 coin win	5
6) 15 coin win	7
7) 20 coin win	10
8) 50 coin win	25

My friend Al Kennkount can't count to 8, even if you spotted him the 1-6. But this math wizard is a dynamite divider and has no trouble seeing the pattern I laid out.

It centers around grabbing approximately 50% of every winning pull. Maybe that seems like a lot of coins to set aside, but what's so wrong about building up that Guarantee?

Al Kenncount may only wanna put aside two or three coins per win, but I kinda disagree with that thought. If you win 25 coins, it just seems kind of senseless to drop one or two coins into your Guarantee cup. Put a decent amount away, at least a third. This way you still keep two-thirds with your Excess.

I use 50% as a guide. I wanna rat-hole approximately 50% of every subsequent win to the Guarantee part of my Session. But the absolute MUST part of this move is putting something aside.

Go back and review this move until you're positive you have it down pat. There's plenty more on this subject coming up...digest the Theory.

8

Play and Run: System #2

Look at the title of this chapter again. It does not say Hit and Run, it says Play and Run. The reason I wanna emphasize that point is because this particular system is pointed right at the people with very short Bankrolls.

If you've gotten this far in the book, it's only fair to assume that you paid attention to some of the things I mentioned about people with short Bankrolls. If you are one of these people, don't feel bad 'cause you got a lotta company.

I can remember times in Las Vegas when a 25¢ Craps game was outta my league 'cause the stakes were too high.

There were also days when I'd be betting 50¢ at a Blackjack table and get dealt a couple of aces vs. the dealer's up card of 5. He was totally in a weak position and the proper move was to split those aces.

But that meant putting an extra 50¢ in action and these were days when I either didn't have that 50¢ or else it was my down payment on supper: a cup of coffee and two donuts w/jelly.

Don't go thinking you're the first player to compete with a Swiss cheese Bankroll (lotta holes in it). So let me give you a system to match your temporary lack of capital.

It ain't geared to give you a jackpot, or allow you to buy a Mercedes on your way home from the casino, or even have you plunk down six months advanced payments on your mortgage.

It's a simple conservative approach that will attempt to increase the $50 Bankroll you started with.

Your bets always start with quarters, and your time at a machine is usually about 4-5 minutes, whether you win or lose. The title tells the whole story: you're gonna play at a lotta machines and you're gonna run, even before your shadow has a chance to settle into position.

Let's say you're walking into a casino with $50 or less and heading for the slots. Break that $50, or whatever you have, into equal Sessions.

Let's say you decide on 10 Sessions of $5 each. You're gonna go to 10 different machines with $5 for each. There is no particular machine you go to, except with this short Bankroll, it must be a quarter machine.

You insert only 25¢ and do not increase your bets. You stay at 25¢ whether you win or lose. Suppose you put in a quarter and get 3 single bars for a return of 10 coins. Next bet 25¢ and you stay at the amount you started with. That means all 10 Sessions (machines) have not more than a 25¢ wager.

You still set Naked Pulls but that is the only Loss Limit imposed. Since your Session amount is so low, the method calls for you to insert the full $5 into the machine, one coin at a time, controlled only by your Naked Pulls figure.

As soon as you have deposited the entire $5 into the machine, and based on the fact the Naked Pulls limit was not reached, that Session is over. You leave that machine as soon as you finish playing that $5.

One thing should be noted: The last pull has to be a Loss. If you put the entire $5 in and the last pull kicked off two cherries, insert another coin. Never let a winning pull be your last pull.

The object is to grind out a short win and run. Since you don't increase your bets, you can't expect the wins to be big. But with the Naked Pulls, the losses won't be heavy.

Suppose you deposited $5 in quarters and ended up with a profit of $1.75. That's the end of the Session. You move to the next machine and continue doing this until all 10 Sessions (or the numbers of Sessions you set up) are finished.

Some Sessions could be winners and others losers, of course, but you're looking for losses to be minimal, while perhaps picking up a couple of dollars profit after all 10 Sessions are done.

Next chapter shows you what to do when all ten Sessions are done. Don't forget, you're starting with a short amount. Get to accept a like result.

9

Chicken System:
System #3

I showed this system in my basic book on Roulette/Slots, so some of you may already know about it.

My friend C. D. Watters couldn't see the river for the water. But he thinks he's the greatest observer of situations since Madam Kon U. Daly opened her Tea Leaf Parlor and promised to tell you everything that was gonna happen over the next five years.

Naturally she cons most people and C. D. Watters is of the same ilk. As soon as he saw the title of this chapter, he screamed: "Oh, I know this system, it don't work!"

Don't listen to cons like Kon U. Daly who'll sell you a different set of bull every day or C. D. Watters, who's usually all wet when it comes to analysis.

All systems work. But all systems do not work all the time. That's why you have stopgaps and Loss Limits to cut losses when a system is going bad.

But systems are approaches with a Disciplined betting pattern, geared to give you a sensible, planned attack at a given machine. To repeat:

1) All systems work.
2) All systems do NOT work all the time.

The Chicken System is an approach geared to give you a planned method at the machine you zero in on. Here's how it works.

You've broken your Bankroll into Sessions, again we'll say 10 Sessions at $10 per machine. But the choice of Sessions is naturally up to you. You've got $10 to invest in the machine you choose.

Again it doesn't matter which machine you select but we'll say it's a three-coin Bar slots. Next thing is the selection of a system and we'll say you decide on the following Series:

a) 1-1-1-2-2-2-3-3-3

You start your series and continue to insert your coins in the prescribed pattern. You set your Naked Pulls at 9, and the Loss Limit is adjusted to 70%.

If your Naked Pulls or Loss Limits is reached, you leave the machine. However, the Chicken approach has a slightly different wrinkle. Unlike the other methods that have you stay at a machine for hours, if your Loss Limits are not reached, the Chicken has a quicker built-in exit.

As soon as you have deposited your entire $10 into the machine, or whatever Session amount you set, you leave that machine. You run like a chicken.

The Session is over as soon as you go through your Session amount. You run like a chicken, whether you are ahead or behind.

In a nutshell, the Chicken System gets you up to a machine, accepts your system, whichever it is, and then calls for you to run like a chicken as soon as your Session amount is deposited once!

a) Set Session amount,

b) Apply System and Series you preset,

c) Set Naked Pulls,

d) Set Loss Limit at 70%,

e) Use entire Session amount (unless Loss Limit or Naked Pulls is reached),

f) Leave machine as soon as all coins are deposited.

When you run like a chicken, you may be ahead and the fact that you must leave that machine is a Disciplined attempt to get you to run with a profit.

Now look at (g) for the list I just gave you. I kept this separate since it is so important:

g) If last coin from your Series was inserted and it was a win, insert coins until loss shows.

The message is obvious. I don't want you leaving a machine on a winning pull. Insert coins until a loss shows and then you leave.

Yeah, it might be a winning Trend but the intent of this method is to get you playing machines and running like a chicken more often.

Go over this approach and then we'll get into offshoots. The Chicken is aiming at a lot of Sessions with the intent of getting a lot of small wins.

10

Chicken System: Squirrel Method: System #4

Before you either accept this method or reject it, at least get to understand its purpose.

The simple intent of the Chicken is to hit and run like a chicken. I happen to like this approach...a lot.

But you gotta remember that I am so involved in Discipline that I got one eye on my Naked Pulls, one eye on my Session amount, to ensure I don't exceed my Loss Limits, and another eye on the credits, to see how the machine is doing.

That leaves me one eye to watch the cocktail waitress coming toward me and the last eye to check out the cocktail waitress walking away—but that's another story.

The main thing is that I use a variation approach to the basic Chicken System called the Squirrel Method. You know how a squirrel will go out and collect goodies and store them away? Well, I use that addition to the Chicken.

I'm still gonna run like a chicken at the end of the insertion of my Session money but there are many times I use the Squirrel addition.

When the Session money, let's say it's $10, is all inserted, we'll assume I'm ahead $4. Take the $10 and put it in your pocket. You can't lose at that machine.

Next take the $4 and break it in half, squirreling away $2 (half) and staying at that machine for an extended time, but only while that extra $2 is being used.

The Squirrel Method makes you wrap up your $10 Session money, so that you cannot lose a dime at that machine. One half of everything you're ahead is rat-holed, guaranteeing a profit, even though it's only a few coins.

It's very similar to my Guarantee and Excess move that you'll be getting a gutful later on, but this time it's done even with tiny profits. You haven't hit a Win Goal and maybe you'll only be up 6 coins.

Being a Chicken, you bury your Session money and 3 coins (.75) and play with the .75 Excess. If you lose that Excess, Session is over.

However, let's say you win 4 coins. Squirrel away 2 coins and add the other 2 to your Excess. Then you win 10 coins on your next pull. Again you squirrel away 5 and add another 5 to the Excess.

See what's happening? As soon as you inserted your entire Session amount into the machine, you act like a chicken. You run, whether you are ahead or not.

But if you adopt the Squirrel addition, it still has you acting like a chicken, by putting away your Session amount.

But if you are ahead, regardless of the amount, you squirrel away half, stay at that machine and continue to squirrel away half of every additional score.

When that Excess is gone, your stay at that machine is over. This is a very conservative approach, hence the words Chicken and Squirrel are used to remind you of that approach.

Naturally the Squirrel addition can only be used if you are ahead, after you finish putting in your Session amount. If there is no profit, you run like a chicken because that's the purpose of this method. The Squirrel addition can **only** be applied if there is a profit to squirrel away.

Then you get into the process of squirreling away half of every subsequent score. I gotta admit that I also like and use this system. I use a lot of small Session amounts which means I can't get hurt at any one machine.

The protection comes from a small Session amount and my Naked Pulls, usually 8. After I insert all of my Session money, if there is a loss, it's surely small. If there is a win, I go into the Squirrel addition.

My friend Don B. Leeve, who doesn't believe in systems, is alarmingly silent. Could it be he's giving some thought to these methods?

Could be! Could be!

11

The Ladder: 3-Coin: System #5

The reason I give names to these systems is so that if you pick one of these approaches, you'll be able to identify the method and zero in on that play or one of it's spin-offs.

I number the systems for reference purposes. This way you can remember the approach by either name or number. The number method helps my friend Ken E. Spell, who cannot spell, so he needs numbers.

On the other hand, my lady friend Miss Dee Kount doesn't know a two from a nine. She missed the count fourteen consecutive years on New Year's Eve, and to this day hasn't got a clue as to what day it is or for that matter what month.

She needs me to give these systems names, 'cause Miss Dee Kount would miss a number reference over and over.

So System #5 will be called the Ladder. It is a perfectly easy Theory to grasp, 'cause the approach is just like going up a ladder: one step at a time.

In fact, it is very close to the Basic System, except that the Ladder Method does not give you the opportunity of staying at a level for periods of time.

The Ladder System always goes up or down by ones and never repeats at any level. You wouldn't wanna stand on any

104

rung of a ladder for long periods unless you were compelled to do so because of a certain job or chore you were doing at a certain level.

But since the basic purpose of the ladder is to go up or down, I use the Theory to keep your bets moving up and down. You go "up" the ladder as you win, you go "down" the ladder as you lose.

Your bets are all tied into Series and there will be many, many Series at each Session. Naturally the obligatory Naked Pulls and Loss Limits apply and I repeat that "Broken Record" message to make sure you never forget it!

The Series always starts in the middle of the Maximum coins required. If you're at a 3-coin machine, your Series starts with 2 coins.

If you're at a 5-coin machine, your Series starts with 3 coins. This way you have the chance to go up if a win occurs and down if a loss is the result.

Suppose you go to a 3-coin machine with $5. Your Loss Limit is 60% and you wanna work the Ladder System.

Your first bet is 2 coins. If you lose, you play 1. If you win, you go back to 2, lose again, go to 1, lose, stay at 1. You win again, go to 2. Again you lose, and must bet 1.

Notice you're reducing your bets after a loss, increasing after a win. When you drop to 1 coin and lose twice, that Series is over and you start again with 3 coins.

By the same token, a few consecutive winning pulls will get you to 3 coins, which would be the maximum. If you bet the 3 coins and win, bet 3 again, win, bet 3 again—a few losses occur and you're down to 1 again. Again you lose at 1: that Series is over.

A new Series has begun and you follow the same pattern. The Series tends to be quick with the Ladder System but the purpose is a controlled way of playing and trying to get you into the habit of winning small amounts consistently.

If you're at a cold machine, the guidelines of Loss Limits will hold those losses way down. Just keep a close watch on your

Session amount and don't exceed the Loss Limits.

This is a snap to grasp. The next chapter touches the 5-coin machines, but you surely should have the pattern down pat by now.

12

The Ladder: 5-Coin: System #6

You already know that the 5-coin machine calls for your Series to start in the middle, with a three-coin shot. A loss calls for a decrease to the next lowest amount.

It's not hard to understand what to bet; my concern is that you grasp the reasons for doing so. In simple logical terms it merely means you bet higher as you win, and bet lower as you lose.

The subsequent bets off the previous play is only affected by single increases or decreases. In other words, a win at the 3 level means your next bet is 4 coins, not a jump to 5. If you lose at the 3-coin play, your next play is 2 coins. You only move one step at a time.

The drawback to this system is obvious and I addressed it in the previous chapter. It has to do with the fact that the Series ends very quickly because as soon as you reach the betting unit of 1 coin and lose, you must go back to the 3-coin Level to begin a new Series. If you keep winning and reach the 5-coin play, let's say another win occurs, stay at 5 coins as long as you keep winning. A loss drops you to 4 coins.

One tiny drawback. Suppose you're in a Series and bet 4 coins and lose. Your next bet must be 3 and again you lose. You bet 2 and lose again! Another blank occurs as you bet one coin, which gives you 4 losses in a row.

You haven't hit your Naked Pulls or Loss Limits so you stay at the machine. But when you get to the end bet in the Ladder System, your Series is over and calls for the start of a new Series.

That means you gotta jump to a 3-Level coin bet, which goes against my basic Theory of betting small as you get into a losing streak.

But the Ladder has its own rules and even though you're in a losing streak of 4 in a row, you jump up to a 3-coin bet.

I realize it ain't like I'm telling you to walk on glass, or eat fire or give up eating for 6 hours, but I am telling you to jump your bet after a loss. It hurts me to make this suggestion but that's the nature of the Ladder System.

My friend Al Sink has taken a close look at this method and sees both the good and bad. "I'll think about it" says Al Sink, which is all I'm asking every one of you to do.

All of these systems are controlled disciplined Money Management moves, presided over by Win Goals and Loss Limits. They are geared to get you away from cold machines and keep you at hot ones.

But most of all they program your every single solitary bet. Therein lies the power of my Theory. Your every move is predetermined with no excuse for error.

So if Al Sink can take the time to think about which system he thinks is best for him, then I think you oughta think about what Al Sink is thinking about and not sink back to your old haphazard way of playing.

I sink it's time to move to the next chapter.

13

Pattern Method: 3 Coin System #7

This system is a little more aggressive, but then a lot of you like that approach. That's all well and good to be aggressive when you're winning, but it sure feeds the ulcer to be betting heavy in the middle of a slump.

Yet many people do that. It's the old "due Theory." I'm due to win. I've already blasted that Theory, so we won't go back over it for awhile.

But I will go over a system called Pattern Method, 'cause you're gonna insert coins in a Pattern that stays constant whether you win or lose.

The Pattern is set up ahead of time, just as you would pre-determine any of your betting methods. It is still done in a Series concept and continues until the Series is completed or you reach your Naked Pulls or Loss Limits. (As the song goes: "There, I've said it again!").

Okay, let's set up some typical Patterns, based on your Session amount:

    a) 1-1-2-2-3-3
    b) 1-1-1-2-2-2-3-3-3
    c) 1-2-3-2-3-4-1-2-3-2-3-4
    d) 2-3-1-2-3-1-2-3-1

e) 3-2-1-3-2-1-3-2-1

f) 1-2-2-3-3-3-2-2-1

g) 1-1-2-2-2-3-3-1-1-2-2-2-3-3

Each of these Series has a Pattern effect. The bets are not affected by the previous decision, as in most of the methods. Instead, you predetermine a Pattern and stay with it throughout the entire Series.

Suppose you decided on Series (e) and inserted 3 coins. You win and now bet 2 coins. Again you win and bet 1 coin. You're betting lower after a win, twice in a row. Then you lose at the one level but the Pattern calls for a 3-coin bet. The system calls for a jump to 3, even though you just had a loss.

It is something like the Ladder, whereby you then must go up with a bet after a loss. Again I remind you of what Discipline and Money Management is. It's a super-controlled approach that doesn't allow you to make decisions, on the chance that they could be dumb decisions.

Notice I point out the bad parts of a system and don't dwell on the good ones. That's because most people are very quick to throw negative reactions back in the face of suggestions.

There will be times you will run into periods where the system you are using will have negative results. I want you to be aware of what to look for and find the drawbacks in a method so you can prepare to wrap up that Session. Plus I positively want you aware that it is important you set up Patterns that you feel comfortable with.

Go back and look at (f) whereby you have a betting sequence of 1-2-2-3-3-3-2-2-1. It has a nice graduated Pattern, sliding up to a 3-coin bet and slowly dropping back to a 2-coin and 1-coin play.

You make your own Patterns or try one that I laid out. Just remember that the maximum amount of plays per Level is five. For instance, you can set up a Series:

h) 1-1-1-1-1-2-2-2-3-3-3-3-3

Five is the max, so even if you win on that last 3-coin bet, you must dive to one and start the Series over again.

One final word before we get deeper. Each bet is made exactly as you laid it out, with no input from the fact that the previous decision was a win or a loss.

14

Pattern Method: 5-Coin: System #8

Again we slide into the offshoot approach at a 5-coin machine, but the Theory remains the same. It just means you have extra Level bets to choose from. Here are some examples:

1) 3-1-3-2-3-3-3-4-3-5
2) 2-1-2-2-2-3-2-4-2-5
3) 1-1-1-2-1-3-1-4-1-5
4) 1-1-2-2-2-3-4-4-4-5-5
5) 1-3-5-5-3-1
6) 2-2-1-1-3-3-1-1-4-4-1-1-5-5
7) 1-2-1-3-1-4-1-5

Look over these variations and see the plus and minus parts to each. Each has a Pattern, each is preset, each includes the conservative coin bet and the aggressive 5-coin bet.

Each Pattern is set to be followed exactly as it was predetermined and yes, each has a strict Loss Limit and Naked Pull application.

You can make the Pattern very aggressive, as long as it doesn't exceed 5 bets at the same amount and you must have a pattern to your Series.

Pattern betting is simply a fancy word for control or Discipline. It makes you approach a machine with a fixed method of betting, a stop Loss and a Win Goal.

The Patterns I set up in the early part of this chapter give you a base to go deeper. Notice that most of them started with one-coin and two-coin inserts.

You know, you can start higher if you like, although for the life of me I can't see why people bet maximum coins at a machine, before finding out if that machine is hot or not.

Yeah, yeah, I know, you wanna hit the Jackpot. But you should also wanna hold losses down and that's the side of the fence I wanna stay on.

But for guys like Imus Pressit, who insist on going for the kill, let me lay out some aggressive Patterns, not because I suggest you use them, but because many of you will do it anyhow, so better I get you realizing you should temper the series (you better):

    a) 5-4-3-2-1-1-2-3-4-5
    b) 5-3-1-1-3-5
    c) 3-4-5-4-3
    d) 2-3-4-5-4-3-2
    e) 3-2-3-3-3-4-3-5-3-4-3-3-3-2

I think you got a grasp of the Pattern approach, whether it be three- or five-coin machines, or for that matter whatever limit machine they may come up with.

At least you'll have a hard-core betting Series to control your play. That's what gambling is about, and that's what Slot playing is all about.

15

Review of Guarantee and Excess

You already know this move, or at least you should. It is designed to rat-hole a profit at every machine where you get ahead. It doesn't take a raving genius to realize what the move is, but it does take a lot of guts to put the exercise into your routine.

The move itself is very simple, the rough part is that it is contrary to how most people play—like dorks!

They get ahead and put the profit back. I was a charter member of the club. There were years when I was in Vegas, back in the sixties, where getting ahead was a piece of cake.

But I ended up getting eaten alive by the casinos 'cause I didn't know how to quit a winner.

It took years to develop and then follow the strict rules of Money Management that I now live and breathe, but the Theory works.

There are a lot of parts to the Theory and you can't break any of the rules, but you'll see how intelligent a move it is when you start leaving the casino with profits.

The two most important things you set at a table are Win Goals and Loss Limits. Notice I didn't say Win Limits. You don't wanna limit wins.

. Loss Limits is a different story. The fraction of an instant you hit your Naked Pulls or Loss Limits, that Session is done. Period!

The instant you hit your Win Goal you also make a move. I asked my friend Bill O. Knee what he does and he gave me a list of things he thought he should do:

His thought:	*My Answer*
1) Leave the Machine!	NO
2) Bet Higher!	NO
3) Bet Lower!	NO
4) Just sit there?	NO
5) Have a drink?	NO
6) Go to the john?	NO
7) Act bored?	NO
8) Cash in for the day?	NO
9) Go to lunch?	NO

Bill O. Knee shouldn't do any of these things and most of all doesn't need to go to lunch 'cause he's already full of baloney. Truth is he doesn't know what to do and all of these things are guesses.

What he should do is take that Win Goal and break it into Guarantee and Excess.

First thing is to rat-hole the Session money, whatever the amount. That way you cannot lose anything at that Session. Next you take that Win Goal, which was a percentage of your Session money and break it in half.

Half goes in your pocket. It is called the Guarantee. You're guaranteed to leave that Session a winner. In this case, one half of whatever your Win Goal was.

The other half is set aside for you to continue playing at that machine, 'cause you're in a hot Trend and I don't wanna see you leaving hot streaks.

The money you set aside to continue playing is your Excess.

There'll be chapters showing you how to handle the Excess. Right now look at this:

1) Set Win Goal at Session,
2) When Win Goal is reached, put aside your Session money,
3) Divide Win Goal in half,
4) Half in your pocket is called Guarantee, never to be touched again that day,
5) Other half you play with. It is called Excess.

Wynn A. Lott is still skeptical, but says he is willing to listen to something that will make him a winner. Listening is one thing. You gotta do it.

On the other hand, Bill O. Knee doesn't like the Theory. He says it restricts him from winning big. No, it doesn't, but he's too full of crazy ideas to see that this move does **NOT** stop you from going for the big score.

All it does is wrap up a guaranteed win and then turns you loose.

Read on... you'll catch the drift.

16

The Regression: System #9

We finally reach the Regression System, a method of betting that has kept me from working for lo these many years. I believe it is the greatest betting system, the strongest Money Management move ever put into use.

This is the eighth book I have written on gambling, and as of this writing there are 23 Video Tapes (on all types of gambling, Craps, Baccarat, Roulette, Blackjack, Pai Gow Poker, Horse Racing, Harness Racing, etc.) and all of these works allude to the Regression System.

Many of you who follow my Theories know how to use it and believe in its use. Those of you who are not familiar with the Regression should pay very, very, very close attention. You will use this method.

In any form of gambling, you have a 50-50 chance of winning or losing. Even if you are a perfect player, know everything about the game you're playing and have all facets of the Big 4, your chances of winning is never better than 50-50.

That's because gambling is set up that way. It's always about 50-50. Take a hand of Blackjack where you are perfect at Basic Strategy. The house has a 1.51% edge on you, which is approximately a 50-50 shot for both player and dealer, with a tiny edge given to the house.

Suppose you're at a Roulette table and decide to play black.

You have 18 numbers that will win for you and 20 numbers won't. In Atlantic City you only lose one half your bet if 0 or 00 shows, so the chance of winning comes to about 18-20 in favor of the house. It's approximately 50-50. It's always 50-50! Never better, so remember that.

Let's say you're playing a hand of Blackjack at a $5 table and your first bet is $10. We'll say you win the $10. Well, you had about a 50-50 chance of winning anyway so it's no big deal.

What the big deal is: what is your next bet? Here is a list of what most people do:

1) Take back $10 and bet $10 again,
2) Take back $5 and go up to $15 bet,
3) Take the $10 win and bet entire $20 on the next hand.

Most people use (1), where they take $10 back and again bet $10. That's called Flat Betting. But you have to win again to show a profit. You have to win 67% of your hands, yet we've already gone over the fact that our chances of winning is only 50-50. Flat betting is a joke. All you do is tread water. Win a few, lose a few. You gotta win way over 50% to show a profit.

Some people use (2). I call them dorks. If they win $10, and then go up to $15 on the next hand and lose, that means they won a hand, lost a hand, which is 50-50 and end up being out $5.

That's crazy. Since your chances of winning is merely 50-50, these poor people accomplished the feat of winning just as many hands as the house (one each), but show a deficit of $5.

The super dork uses (3). He bets $10, wins, and lets the whole $20 ride. If he loses, he is out $10, while winning one hand and losing one hand.

Sure, it's great if you win that second hand, but then you are fighting the 50-50 odds factor.

So what's the proper move? I say use the Regression system. Bet $10 and if you win, immediately swing into your Money Management move:

1) Take back the $10 you started with, now you have no risk,
2) Also take back one half of that $10 win for a guaranteed $5

profit,
3) Bet $5 on the next hand. Even if you lose that $5 bet, you
   have your original $10 wager plus a $5 profit.

You won just as many hands as the dealer (one each), yet you
have a profit of $5 so far. I ain't asking you to stop eating for 6
days, or walk on hot coals or stop cheating on your wife or go to
church once a week, or give up any other such rotten habits
your have.

All I'm asking you to do is play the house even and end up
with a little profit for that 50-50 standoff.

The Regression System does that. It gives you a profit by
making you "regress" after the first win, lock up that profit and
then revert to "Up and Pull."

We'll get into that, but for now take a good
looooooooooooooooonnnnnnnnnnnggggggggggggg loook at this
Theory.

17

Understanding the Regression

The previous chapter explained the Theory of Regression. I want you to understand how powerful the move is, so before you either condone or condemn the method, get to understand what it is all about.

First of all, you must bet higher than the minimum so you have room to Regress. If you're at a $5 table, then your first bet must be either $10, $9, $8, $7, or $6. It gives you room to go down and lock up a profit.

We'll say $7 is your first bet. If you win that $7 bet, do the following:

a) Take back original $7 wager.

b) Take back $2 profit, leaving $5 as your next bet.

c) Even if you lose that $5 bet, you have a $2 profit for that Series with another $7.

d) Suppose you win that first $7 bet, regress to a $5 bet. You win gain. Revert to "Up and Pull."

e) Take back a profit, any profit and continue betting. Say you take back a $2 profit. That leaves you $8 as your next bet.

f) If you lose, Series is over and another Series starts with a $7 bet.

g) However, if you won at the $8 bet, Series is still alive and

120

you're into "Up and Pull."

h) Dealer pays you $8. Go up to $10 and pull back $6. Or go up to $11 and pull back $5. Or go up to $12 and pull back $4. But pull back **something.** I don't give a rat's tail how much, just as long as you pay yourself.

See how simple and rewarding it is? You're upping your bets and grabbing a profit after *every* win. A loss wraps up that Series and you start over.

The whole key was in the move you made after the first win. You went down! You Regressed, locked up a profit and put yourself in a plus position. Every subsequent win gives you a few dollars more.

I ain't gonna belabor the method as it applies to Blackjack or Craps or Roulette but you get the idea. If you wanna go deeper into the application of the Regression at the table games, go look at the tapes and book.

I wanna show you how to apply the Regression to the Slots.

18

Regression in Slots

Now you know what the Theory of the Regression is: Regress your bet after the first win, lock up a profit and then go to Up and Pull.

What you wanna know now is how the Regression System can be applied to Slots. Good question, glad you asked. Actually, the Regression was designed to be used at even money payoffs such as Blackjack, outside bets of Roulette, Baccarat, Baseball, Basketball, Football and to the place numbers in Craps.

In Slots there are multiple-coin payoffs such as 3 coins for two Cherries, 10 coins for any three Bars, 14 coins for three Oranges, etc., etc., etc.

But the Theory is so powerful that it is possible to apply it to the Slots. You can use it at either the three- or five-coin machines but the five are better.

Break your Bankroll into Sessions and go to a machine. Yeah, you gotta set Win Goals, Loss Limits and Naked Pulls so don't even ask.

If you go to this system of the Regression, your first bet has to be higher than the minimum, even though it's not an even money payoff.

Your first bet is two coins. If you lose, two coins, if you lose, two coins. If you win, take your payoff or let the credits accumulate, whichever you choose, but instead of again betting two coins, or moving to three, your next bet regresses to 1 coin. If you lose, the Series is over and you return to a new Series and bet 2 coins.

Suppose you won at the two-coin insertion and dropped to one coin and won again. You're in a Series and the Up and Pull Theory now takes hold. As long as you keep winning, please keep increasing until you reach maximum coins and stay at max. Whenever a loss occurs, the Series is over and you begin again, using two coins as your start, regressing to one after a win and going up in your bets as you continue to win.

Lay out your Series beforehand, pick a system and stick to it. Your Loss Limits will protect you, but not if you're a crazy bettor.

Try the Regression System, starting with 2 coins. If you win, regress down to 1, then 2, then 3, then 4, then stay at 5 as long as you keep winning. A loss signals the start of a new Series.

The next chapter goes into offshoots but that's only to give you different sets of Series. This chapter gives you a basic approach, and what's so bad about putting in 2 coins, winning 10 and cutting back to 1?

Notice how this system goes down after a win and some of the others go up after a win. It's all in the Theory you believe in and the method you feel most comfortable with.

Just remember:
1) The Regression starts higher than the minimum coins required,
2) After the first win, you regress to the minimum bet,
3) As you win, you go up one betting level at a time (2-3-4-5 coins),
4) As soon as a loss occurs, go back to first bet of the Series and start over.

Don't stop here, the Regression carries over to the next chapter, so don't lose the drift.

19

Regression: 3-Coin: System #10

The whole basis of the Regression System is to bet higher than the minimum and then regress down to the table minimum after a win. But you can carry that Theory too far. My reason for using it is to keep people playing conservative so they don't get whacked in the casinos.

My friend Guy S. Weiss is a wise guy. He likes to bust my chops by taking my conservative approach and turning it into a barn burner. He tells me he'll use the Regression, then makes $100 his first bet and his regression move down to $50 after a win.

Guy S. Weiss is not as wise as he thinks. His Bankroll is usually $200, he bets like his chips were grenades ready to go off in his pockets and he loses more often than he wins 'cause he won't quit when he's ahead.

He knows his aggressive style turns me off so he does it just to be a wise guy. His mother had 7 Weiss guys, but this jerk is the only one who ain't so smart, if you catch my drift.

One time I asked him: "If you bet $100 and after a win, dive down to $50, what is your potential winning margin?"

Immediately he answers "Fifty dollars, 'cause if I lose the $50 bet, I still have a $50 profit." He smirks at me with that "I know it all" cockiness! So I ask him another question: "What is your potential loss?" Again, he spits out $100. Again he's right. He could lose $100 but if he wins that first hand, he has a guaranteed $50 socked away.

So I say to him: "Hey, Weiss guy, why risk $100 as your first bet and then go down to $50? Sure, you have a locked up-profit of $50 but a possible loss of $100. Why don't you start with a $55 bet and if you win, regress down to a $5 bet. This way you have a potential profit of $50 for a win. However, with my way you can only lose $55, and yours, you can lose $100."

Guy S. Weiss looked at me, unable to answer, 'cause there was no answer this guy could give. Why bet so high for the same possible profit margin? It's better if you bet lower but keep the spread the same. Cuts down the amount of the possible first loss.

In Slots you don't get single-coin payoffs, as the returns tend to be greater because of the multiple coin kickoff.

But since there is a multiple-coin kickoff, you're getting a decent payoff for 2 coins, so why put the extra risk on your shoulder by betting higher amounts?

If you like the Regression and wanna get a little more aggressive than a 2-1-3-4-5 betting Series, let's look at a start with 3 coins:

   a) 3-2-3-4-5
   b) 3-1-2-3-4-5
   c) 3-1-1-2-2-3-3
   d) 3-2-1-1-2-3-4-5
   e) 3-2-2-3-3-4-4-5-5
   f) 3-1-2-1-3-1-4-1-5
   g) 3-1-2-2-3-3-3-4-4-4-4
   h) 3-1-1-3-3-5-5
   i) 3-2-2-3-3-4-4-5-5

Those are just a few examples, starting with a 3-coin insertion and applying the Regression Theory. You can come up with a variation of a 3-coin start. But just remember to preset your Series and don't deviate from it until you wrap up that Session.

Next chapter we wrap up this approach but I think you see the plus side.

20

Step System: System #11

This is a method which is a spin-off of several of the prior systems, such as the Ladder. Just like all the others, it has a predetermined Series of bets which control how much you wager at each level.

In the Step System you do not increase or decrease bets after a win or loss, you stay at your prescribed system for the time period you already setup.

This can be used at either a 3-coin or 5-coin machine. You decide if you are a conservative or aggressive player and then make out your Series. You will stay at a betting level for X number of pulls, all of which you will decide upon before you enter the casino.

Starting with the basic bet of one coin, you decide how long you wanna deposit one coin at a time, with no factor given to whether it was a win or loss.

We'll say you wanna begin with one coin for 5 pulls, then graduate to two coins for 5 pulls, and so on. Here's how you'd lay out your Sessions:

a) 1-1-1-1-1
b) 2-2-2-2-2
c) 3-3-3-3-3

d) 4-4-4-4-4
e) 5-5-5-5-5

Simple, ain't it? Just as simple as walking up a flight of steps. You stay at one coin for however many plays you feel comfortable with, then move to the next step. Stay there for the same number of plays, then move on. But you gotta have each Series set ahead of time.

A lot of times you won't hit the end of the Series because your Loss Limits will make you wrap up a Session, or your Naked Pulls pops up.

No, you cannot waive the Naked Pulls limit because you have a feeling the next pull will be the bonanza. And yes, you will be mad because sometimes you'll have to leave three, four or five Sessions in a row due to those Loss Limits.

And yes, I understand your frustrations; but no, I won't allow you to alter one tiny little thing. And finally, yes, I know you will break the rules and you'll know that I know that no amount of excuses will offset the fact you also know that somehow I'll know that you know that I know and yes, when I meet you, the look in your eye will give away the fact that you know that I know that you know that I know, but that's another story....

The story we're into now has to do with the Step System. The Series I laid out is very basic, so here is another couple of Series you may want to use.

a) 1-1-1
b) 2-2-2
c) 2-2-2
d) 3-3-3
e) 3-3-3
f) 3-3-3
g) 4-4-4-4
h) 4-4-4-4
i) 4-4-4-4
j) 4-4-4-4

Each step has the number of pulls to correspond with the number of coins you will insert. Note that the Step System does not use Regression moves, by going down after a win or loss. It just moves to the next step.

The previous table stopped after four plays with 4 coins at each of 4 levels. At that point, if your Loss Limits have not kicked in, you can go on to five plays at 5 coins each for 5 straight Levels. Or after the 4 coin plays, you may wanna drop to the one factor and start all over.

This is all determined ahead of time and not when you reach the end of a particular step. Or have I said that before?

More on the Step System coming up. Once you have grasped the basic Theory, you may proceed.

21

Step System: 3-Coin: System #12

The first chapter on the Step System went right to the 5-coin machine but I already made it clear that you can apply this approach to a 3-coin slot.

Here are some examples:

a) 1-1-1

b) 2-2-2

c) 3-3-3—then start over

That's so easy, even Watt E. Cey is smiling. It's the first system he got on the first look.

Since we're at only a 3-coin machine, the lesser amount of combinations may hinder the aggressive player, but just stay longer at each step. The key to remember with the Step is that you can't go back down the steps until you reach the last step and that means the final pull on the last stage of the last step. Then you go back down the steps and start all over again.

There is no betting when you go down the steps. You just start all over and go back up—one step at a time.

Don't worry, the next chapter will have you going down the steps, but for now just look at going up at 3-coin machines.

This example keeps you longer at each step and you can spread it out any way you like:

a) 1-1-1
b) 2-2-2
c) 2-2-2
d) 2-2-2
e) 3-3-3
f) 3-3-3
g) 3-3-3
h) 3-3-3

That last example can be changed in all sorts of directions to longer or shorter stays at each step. Just keep the betting sequences in a 1-2-3 format.

Finally, you could look at a very conservative Step Series, where the emphasis is on the one-coin insertion, instead of at the top of the steps, where 3 coins are used.

a) 1-1-1
b) 1-1-1
c) 1-1-1
d) 2-2-2
e) 2-2-2
f) 3-3-3—Start over at 1

Sure, there'll be times you'll win early with the one coin plays but that's the way the bell bangs. You wouldn't be mad if the losses were at the one-level play and the wins at the three-level play.

Then you'd be saying what a great guy I am for getting you to the hot winnings at just the right time. But if you didn't have something to complain about, you wouldn't be human.

My friend Ken Plane can't spit out five consecutive words without complaining about something.

Once I saw him at the casinos in Vegas and he was having a bad night at the Slots. I took him to a group of quarter machines and had him play the Basic Stagger Method.

Within a half hour he won 3 jackpots and was a half skip and jump away from dropping on both knees and kissing my feet. He wanted to give me half his winnings but stopped short of that statement, as he started to turn blue and almost choked on the words. But he was overcome with joy and skipped off into the night praising my patron saint, St. Patrick and everyone who bore that name, figuring we were all direct descendants.

The next day I happened to see him squatting on the rail of a bridge, getting ready to jump. I inquired as to why he was so upset and wasn't so happy about winning three jackpots the night before!

He replied through a wailing and gnashing of teeth: "Yeah, I was happy until I got home and my wife told me that about the same time as I was winning, a guy in her section of the casino was winning 5 jackpots. So I appreciate all you did for me, Patrick, but I might have been at those machines!"

Ken Plane doesn't have anything to complain about since that day on the bridge. No, he didn't jump. I pushed!

22

Down the Steps Method: System #13

There are a lot of phrases we live with:
1) Time marches on.
2) For every good woman there's gotta be a good man (but there ain't).
3) Laugh and the world laughs with you.
4) Everything good happens to he who waits.
5) A watched pot never boils.
6) What goes up must come down.

None of these things apply to gambling, except (6) and that's because we're talking about the Step System where I told you to go up one step at a time: bet one coin, then two coins, then three coins, etc.

So the saying could have something to do with this system and since we've gone up the steps, I think we oughta put in a system of coming down the steps.

'Cause as they say: "What goes up must come down!" Lying in bed the other night I was thinking about that saying and how it doesn't always apply to just the way it sounds.

What if you're a deep-sea diver, then the opposite is true: "What goes down must come up!"

Let's go to the Step System and we'll start at the top of a

Series for the 3-coin machine. This time you lay out bets starting with the max and work down the steps:

a) 3-3-3
b) 2-2-2
c) 1-1-1

(Then start over.)

Or you could spread out the plays at each step, while at the same time working backward:

a) 3-3-3
b) 3-3-3
c) 2-2
d) 2-2
e) 1-1
f) 1-1

With this approach, controlled as it is, your initial bets are higher and you end up playing at lesser amounts as you go deeper into the Series. There are good and bad points to every approach. Let's examine this particular one:

Bad Point: You may start off losing at the 3-coin play and end up playing only single coins when machine gets hot.

Bad Point: You may be winning at the 3-coin play and have the Series force you into lower plays as it gets hot.

Both of these complaints are valid. Let's go to the good point:

Good Point: You may start off winning with 3-coin play and when reach lower bets you may be losing smaller amounts,

You see how dumb it is when you end up having hindsight at a Session? Of course, all of the above is true. But you ain't gonna know which way the machine will Trend. That's why I give you stop points.

There will be times when all of the above will happen. You'll be jumping back and forth being happy and sad, depending on whether you are winning or losing. Or you'll blame me and anyone else you can think of for having you set up such a Series.

If you play the Step System, decide if you wanna start at the bottom and work up the steps or start at the top and work down the steps. Then, when you decide, lay out the plays at each step and stick to it.

I guess I believe in the saying "What goes up must come down." But I think:

a) I see smoke go up but never see it come down.

b) I see prices go up but rarely see them come down.

c) I see my waistline going up, never see it coming down.

Maybe everything that goes up doesn't come down. How about Dolly Parton.... Well, that's another story!

23

The Shotgun:
System #14

You know the damage a shotgun can do. It spreads bullets all over the place, hitting not only the broad side of a barn but the outhouses on both sides, and the back side of an old bull minding his own business a hundred feet away from the barn.

That's the good part of the shotgun—it spreads the scores all over the place. But it also has a bad side. When it does hit something, the bullets spray so much that very little damage is done.

The broad side of the barn has only a few holes in it and even the outhouse doesn't crumble under the spray.

Of course if you tell that old bull that the buckshot hanging out of his behind really doesn't hurt, you'll get his version of a soft-shoe number, which he'll gladly perform on the part of your anatomy where the sun don't shine.

But all in all, the shotgun has some instances where it scores a lot, but not often enough, if you catch my drift.

So the System we'll go over now is called the Shotgun. That's because you're gonna take a shot at a row of machines, where you won't do a lot of damage, but you may get a number of small hits.

We'll say you have a $20 Session amount and pick a row of

machines, maybe 6, where you'll put your plan into play.

Actually, you're taking a shot at all 6 machines, not just one, hoping one of them is ripe for a score. You set up your patterns of play and in this System it's not aimed at just one machine, but how much you'll put into each of the machines. We'll start with the first machine where you deposit one, then two, then three coins. Then move onto the next machine, except if the three-coin play kicks off a score. In that instance you gotta repeat the amount of coins you played, in this case 3, 'cause you *never* leave a machine where your last play was a winning one.

Or have I said that... yes I have. I've said it before!

Each machine of the 6 you picked out gets the same level play. In this case we went 1-2-3. If it is a 5-coin machine (and they all gotta be the same), then you'd go 1-2-3-4-5. Then all the machines of the group gets 1-2-3-4-5.

Even my foreign friend from France, Count de Kennot III, who does most of his gambling in Monte Carlo, can't count the number of toes he has on both feet, but he has mastered the art of counting to 5.

That's all he needs to make this system work. You pick the 6 machines, arrive at a Session amount, lay out your Series and go right down the line. It's as easy as 1-2-3-4-5.

1) Pick 6 machines.
2) Set aside 15 coins for each.
3) Set Naked Pulls and Loss Limits.
4) Deposit coins in the pattern you set up (1-2-3-4-5).
5) When the 6 machines have been played, Series is finished.
   Go back and start over.

Even if Count de Kennot III cannot count the number of wives he has, these 5 steps will be easier for him to remember.

The Shotgun Theory is that one, two or even three of those machines will kick off a return. The most you are investing in a machine is the total of the Series (1-2-3-4-5) equals 15 coins or $3.75 per machine at the quarter Slots or $7.50 at the 50¢ Slots. Your Bankroll will decide what amount machine you'll play. You know I'm gonna suggest the lowest one.

If you have a small stake, simply cut down your Series to 1-2-3. That means at a quarter Slots you're risking $1.50 per machine and $9.00 for the whole group of six machines. You can use this Series with a $10 Session amount.

The Shotgun gives you a couple of shots at several machines. You ain't gonna win a lot of money at one machine but you won't do too much damage to your Bankroll.

24

The Shotgun: Conservative Approach: System #15

There are variations to this system, as you can play the Shotgun at 3 machines or 4-5-6-8-10, whatever number you want. You can also use any number of coins and your choice of a Series.

The previous chapter gave you an introduction to the method. I used six machines with a 1-2-3 pattern. That approach ain't the best you'll ever see, nor is it the worst. It is merely an example that you can use, change or improve upon.

The Shotgun also can go all the way down to three machines, where you insert a 1-1-1 Series of coins. Or you could take 10 machines and use the Regression Series of 4-3-2-4-5. Hey, that's a heavy layout of coins at ten machines.

The previous paragraph went to the extremes with the Shotgun, showing you a tiny fragment of a bullet and a rat-a-tat-tat of gunfire. That's because there's so much room for variations, not just in the amount you bet per Series, but because you're taking on multiple machines.

The last chapter was a middle of the road approach, but in this chapter we'll drop down to a conservative approach. Again I warn you, which is another term for "I demand you," to play within the parameters of your own personal Bankroll.

Maybe one of the aggressive Series will appeal to you. It'll look so enticing and so temptingly productive that you'll be swayed to take on 8 machines with a 1-2-2-3-3-3-4-4-4-5-5-5 Series.

You're positive that this is your day, even though you know that your arsenal contains only a half-loaded pea-shooter, which amounts to about a $75 total Bankroll. You decide to go for the heavy Series, even though you're playing with a short stake. Wrong! I don't care how good the method looks, if you don't have the bread you can't make a sandwich. You don't have the money, you can't play heavy.

I'll give you a conservative approach that can be used with a $10 Session amount, spread over 4 machines. That'll get you started.

It doesn't matter if the 4 machines are all next to each other or every other machine or on opposite sides of the row. Just pick 4 machines that you like. With a $10 Session amount, use either the 1-2-3-4-5 Series I showed you in the previous chapter or slide over to one of these:

1) 2-2-1-1-2-2-1-1
2) 1-2-1-2-1-2-1-2
3) 1-1-2-2-3-3-2-2-1-1
4) 1-2-3-3-2-1

You'll recognize each of these Series as a Pattern Method. The bets range from 1 to 3 coins at each of the 4 machines, so your chances of getting clobbered is remote.

Naturally you can work out your own Series, being even more conservative. Spread your play over the number of machines you desire. Maybe you'll wanna use 3 machines, maybe you'll go for a whole row of 8 machines.

It doesn't matter, as long as you stay within your Session amount. One other tiny thing that I'd like to address.

You do not use the Shotgun to go for the big return. Sure, it'll be nice to land at a machine just as the R.N.G.'s spit out a bonanza, but don't set your heart and soul on it.

You're using the Shotgun to try and pick up a couple of coins per machine and hope that you're fortunate to have at least 50% of the machines you choose banging out a return—regardless of the amount.

This is the conservative approach to the Shotgun and I think you'll see how easy it is. Once you've played the amount of machines you decided upon and played out the Series at each, that Session is over.

The next Session starts with a whole new bank of machines. You don't replay the same ones unless you predetermined to do so, based on a certain profit.

This approach is different from a lot of the systems that keep you at the same machine. Here you go to a group of machines and apply a Hit and Run Theory.

But... but... but if you predetermined (and that's the key term) to repeat at the same machines in the event of a profit, then that you *can* do!

25

Umbrella System:
System #16

The last chapter was a longie but that's because I wanted to get across the message that these systems are not geared to make you rich. They are strictly a tool to control every single solitary bet you make. No longer will you just pop coins in, without a preset pattern or system to guide you.

Speaking of systems, here's one called the Umbrella, due to the fact that the bets always start small, work up to a long run at maximum coins and then work back down to smaller ones.

Sure, it's "just another pattern" but it does interest both the small bettor and the aggressive player, 'cause you can adjust how much you play at each Level. But remember, the absolute maximum amount of coins you can bet at any one Level is 5.

Here are some sample Series:
a) 1-1-3-3-3-5-5-4-4-4-2-2
b) 1-1-1-4-4-5-5-5-3-3-2-2-2
c) 1-1-4-4-5-5-5-3-3-2-2
d) 1-1-1-1-3-3-3-5-5-5-4-4-4-2-2-2-2
e) 1-4-4-5-5-5-3-3-2
f) 1-1-3-3-5-5-5-4-4-2-2

Take a look at the patterns for the Umbrella System. Surely you've picked up the basic purpose by now. It's in the fact that the bets start small and work up to the max of 5 and stay there for 3, 4 or 5 pulls and then start back down to the 2-coin pull.

Look at those examples. Notice that you can creep up to the 5-coin max and then stay there for 3-4-5 pulls before dropping down.

You can also employ patterns whereby you use the same Theory of getting to the max and then repeating the same pattern back down to the minimum play.

Take a look:

a) 1-2-3-4-5-5-5-4-3-2-1
b) 1-1-3-3-5-5-3-3-1-1
c) 1-1-2-2-3-3-4-5-4-3-3-2-2-1-1
d) 1-1-3-3-5-5-3-3-1-1
e) 1-1-2-4-5-5-4-2-1-1
f) 1-1-1-3-4-5-5-5-5-4-3-1-1-1

Notice every Series starts small and after reaching the max amount, comes right down to the first bet, with equal play amounts on either side of the maximum bet.

None of the Series aimed for the 5-coin play, stayed a while and then slid back down.

So I'll give you a couple:

a) 1-1-2-3-4-5-5-5-5-5-4-3-2-1-1
b) 1-2-2-3-5-5-5-5-3-2-2-1
c) 1-1-3-4-5-5-5-5-4-3-1-1
d) 1-1-2-3-4-4-5-5-5-5-4-4-3-2-1-1

This is not a bad approach 'cause it works up to the max bet and stays there for a couple of pulls.

The drawback is that you keep going up with your bets, regardless of the results of the previous pull. For instance, look at (b) above. After 4 pulls you're in the max territory of 5 coins for 4 straight pulls.

You have your Loss Limits and Naked Pulls to protect you but the fact that you're betting 5 coins after 4-5 losses can be expensive. Try this method with a Series that starts off with a string of one-coin bets and goes up slowly. The Series could be long, but if it cuts losses, what could be wrong with it:

a) 1-1-1-1-2-2-3-5-5-5-3-2-2-1-1-1-1

Start with a Series like this one, or even more conservative if that's your choice. But the approach has merit!

If after the Series ends and you have a profit for that Session, revert to the Guarantee and Excess Theory. Rat-hole a profit, which is your Guarantee and proceed at the same machine with the Excess.

You say you don't understand the Guarantee and Excess? Then get your hide back to those chapters and learn it.

NOW!

26

Senior Citizen Gamblers

Don't fluff past this chapter, 'cause it has a direct impact on anyone reading this book. The message is aimed at the Senior Citizen but you apply if one of the following categories fits your situation:

a) You're a Senior Citizen.
b) You know a Senior Citizen.
c) You take a parent or relative who is a Senior Citizen to the casinos.
d) You've heard of a person who is a Senior Citizen.
e) You are approaching Senior Citizen status.
f) You've heard the term Senior Citizen.
g) You're 21 years old or older and eventually will become a Senior Citizen.

If you qualify for any one of these categories, you should read this chapter.

The Senior Citizen is the backbone of this country from a standpoint of spending money and the casinos are packed with them every day. Atlantic City is a fabulous outlet for them because of the number of Seniors who are bussed in every day.

Las Vegas and points west do a booming business with the Seniors because of the lure of vacations, so getting the Senior Citizen gambling dollars is a big thing for all the casinos.

But the thing that irritates me the most is the Senior Citizen herself or himself. I hate the "poor me" syndrome they put themselves in. I talk to hundreds of Seniors each week and they all tell me they don't play the table games 'cause they're intimidated and scared of the noise and other players.

Can you imagine that nonsense? You could take a hundred Senior Citizens, ship them to Iraq and they could have ended that war in a matter of hours.

They got more brass gall than a bowl of tin monkeys. I know! I give seminars in Senior Citizen centers all over the state. Shrinking violets they ain't... except when they enter a casino, and hide behind the facade that they're "afraid" of the table games.

They're trying to use their so-called advanced age as a wall that they put up when they feel intimidated by a situation. Maybe you do the same thing or intend to use the same ploy when you reach that designation.

I believe Senior Citizens should learn to play Craps, Roulette, Baccarat, Pai Gow Poker, and any of those casino games where the house edge is not as steep as it is in Slots playing.

But for those Seniors who won't play the table games and insist on hiding in the Slots section, at least heed the advice I give you on Money Management.

Don't hide behind the excuse you're "too old to learn new games," or "too old to change old habits." If you persist on playing the Slots, try these Money Management moves and systems. They give you an intelligent approach, regardless of your age.

For you people who hide behind the "age factor," get over it. You can always learn new games and you can always improve the way you play the Slots.

You ain't as old as you try to pretend.

27

Elastic System: System #17

Let's get back to a few more Systems, before we forget that you gotta have a plan of attack when you reach those machines.

Hope you're already zeroed in on a few of the ones that were laid out for you, but if not, here is one that could be either a primary play or even a back-up to the ones you've already decided on.

It's called the Elastic System, 'cause you're gonna spread your bets out in a type of stretching fashion.

Naturally you always wanna start with a small bet, so that your losses are minimal. But you'd also like to get to the increases, in the event the machine warms up. This System gives you long Series but is very flexible, allowing moves toward the max bets.

Notice in these Series that you strettttccccchhhhh your bets out little by little and of course you can eventually get them to the higher plays:

A) 1-1-2-2-1-1-3-3-1-1-4-4-1-1-5-5

If Naked Pulls or Loss Limits are not hit, start over.

B) 1-1-1-2-2-1-1-1-3-3-1-1-1-4-4

C) 1-1-2-1-1-3-1-1-4-1-1-5-1-1

D) 1-2-1-3-1-4-1-5-1-4-1-3-1-2

E) 1-1-1-2-2-1-1-1-3-3-1-1-1-4-4

F) 1-2-3-1-2-4-1-2-5

Remember your Loss Limits and Naked Pulls still apply but if you reach the end of a Series, go back and start over with the same Series.

Once you completely understand the Theory of Guarantee and Excess, you can get more aggressive with your Series, **AFTER** you hit your Win Goal and divide that profit into your Guarantee and Excess.

Then and only then can you start to step up your play with higher coin insertions. If you don't understand the Guarantee and Excess exercise, flip back to those chapters and devour the information.

Rhee Repeet wants me to go over those moves again, but that's only because she's too lazy to read those chapters again. Well, I ain't repeating the message, 'cause at the time I broke it down, it was made very clear that it was one of the biggest moves in your day.

If you also forgot it, then follow Ivor Gott back through time until you all grasp the Theory.

The Elastic System is conservative because it always reverts back to one coin, but that's because so many people play with only $10 or less per machine. For those of you in that category, these Series are for you.

If you have a bigger Bankroll, then the next chapter may have a Series that tickles your fancy.

28

Elastic Aggressive: System #18

Since I am such a conservative gambler, I get eight new gray hairs every time I use the word *aggressive*. It's because I know how hard it is to win at gambling, that I cringe when I tell you people that now you can become more aggressive. It's against my instincts to do this.

I then picture a hundred people flying into the casino, playing six machines at once, using maximum coins and signing a $1,000 marker with their left foot, so as not to miss a pull.

My idea of aggressive is to call Racquel Welch on the phone twice a week instead of once. Heck, two No's are worse than one, but a devil of a lot better than eighteen.

So if you let it all hang out by betting aggressive, you're wide open for a lot of losing Sessions. When I say aggressive, it means go up with your bets, but go up slowly.

So let's go a little up with a couple of Series, utilizing the Elastic approach:

    a) 1-2-2-3-3-3-4-4-4-4
    b) 2-3-4-4-5-5-5
    c) 2-2-3-3-3-4-4-4-5-5-5
    d) 2-3-1-4-5-1-2-3-1-4-5-1
    e) 2-2-3-3-3-4-4-5-5-5

f) 1-1-2-2-2-3-3-3-3-1-1-2-2-2

Notice that this system does not call for a jump to the maximum coins after a hit, although several prior systems did allow for that situation.

That's an aggressive approach. At lectures I give on gambling, there is mixed feelings about jumping to the max bet after a hit. Sure, the only way you're gonna win the big one is by putting in max coins. But if your Bankroll doesn't allow it, why put yourself in a position of going broke early!

How many jackpots have you won right up to this moment, for amounts exceeding $5,000? Remember, you had to put in maximum coins!

Yet how many of those days would have been winning trips, if you played small and just increased your bets in slow progressions?

To properly use the Elastic, always start with one or two coins and slowly stretch out your bets, always staying with your pre-determined pattern, whether you lost or won on the previous pull.

You may not like the similarity between systems, from a standpoint of setting up your Series. That's because there are a lot of spin-offs from the basic Series right up to super-aggressive moves.

You may crisscross a Series from another system and that's perfectly okay. It merely means the duplicate Series seems interesting enough to pop into your brain again. You wanna use that Series.

Look at the Elastic System. Write out your own Series, even going way way down to super-conservative:

a) 1-1-1-1-2-2-2-2-3-3-3-3-4-4-4-4-5-5-5-5

Nothing wrong staying at a certain level for multiple pulls but predetermine it. Or have I . . . Oh, forget it!

29

Hi-Lo System:
System #19

Most of these Systems are self-explanatory because the title gives away the Theory. This system is no different. In fact my friend Hy O'Solow has already worked it out. He screams out the Theory: "You bet high and then you bet low." Then pops his chest out for being so smart.

If this raving genius Hy O'Solow can pick it up so quickly, then all of you should be in the same boat. This will keep you zeroed in on the system of your choice by remembering its moves as explained by the title.

Yet this is a system that starts high and works down to low but there is a key move to the system that Hy O'Solow did not explain. It has to do with a preset number that keeps you dropping to a lower bet, when the machine gets into a cold or losing pattern.

Be sure you understand this whole system before you play, because there ain't room for mistakes in gambling. As I said before, the perfect player has only a 50-50 chance of winning—there is no room for error.

In this system you start at the maximum bet, assuming you have the Session amount to allow the high level bet. The Series will be laid out to start your bets high but since I am so adamant

151

about holding losses down, I want you to set a key number of 3-4-5, whereby if you go that many Naked Pulls without a score, you drop to the next lowest level.

Let's say you set 3 as your key back-up Naked Number. This is not to be confused with your regular Naked Pulls limit, where you must leave the machine if your Naked Pulls of 7-8-9-10 or whatever you set shows up.

This Naked Number pertains only to the number of blank returns you get at a certain Level bet.

Suppose you have your Naked Number at 3 and start your Series with 5 coins. If you get 3 blanks in a row, even though you set five coins for 5 pulls, you have to leave that coin limit and drop to the next lowest bet, which would be 4 coins. Suppose you set your Series as follows:

a) 5-5-5-5-5-4-4-4-4-4-3-3-3-3-3-2-2-2-2-2-1-1-1-1-1

You start off playing five coins and the first three pulls are losses. You must drop to a four-coin play. Your Series has you playing four coins for 5 pulls, but your Naked Number was hit, so you gotta drop your bets to the next lowest Level. You're then allowed 5 plays at the four-coin amount, unless three in a row result in losses. If that happens, you regress to the three-coin Level.

The next chapter allows longer plays per Level, as we recognize the higher heeled player, but to understand this play, remember you're still in the 5-play move per level.

b) 5-5-5-5-5-3-3-3-3-3-1-1-1-1-1-4-4-4-4-4-2-2-2-2-2

c) 5-5-5-5-5-4-4-4-4-4-5-5-5-5-5-3-3-3-3-3-2-2-2-2-2

d) 5-5-5-5-4-4-4-4-2-2-2-2-5-5-5-5-3-3-3-3-1-1-1-1

Again I remind you of the amount of coins you need per Session, so go back to the chapters on Sessions and make sure you qualify for the playing of maximum coins. Then you can lay out your Series that start with higher betting amounts, such as 5 coins, but for only a certain amount of plays.

All of the previous Series started with maximum coin insertions and worked down, but some of them have stagger series.

The Naked Number is just an added guide to get you to lower your bets when things start to cool down. That's in line with my Theory to bet lower when losing.

You can set your Naked Number at 2 if you like or go to 3 or 4, wherever you feel comfortable.

After the Series is completed and your Naked Pulls or Loss Limit was not reached, you start the Series over.

This is a good approach for the heavier Bankrolled player, and just to give you a few spin-offs, the next chapter shows variations and then longer Series.

One final point: The three-coin machine also qualifies for this play, and that will also be covered after we finish with the five-coin.

30

Hi-Lo Aggressive: System #20

Before you forget this Theory, let's glide right into an aggressive application of the Hi-Lo System.

But first of all let me give you a change that has not been applied to any of the previous Systems. Up to now you had a limit of 5 plays at any one-coin Level.

That means if you set a Series at 2-2-2-2-2-2-3-3-3-4-4-4 you could not do it. The two-coin Level shows 6 plays and that is a no-no!

I incorporated a max of five plays at every level to stop the aggressive non-disciplined player from bending the rules and setting up two plays at one coin and eight plays at 5 coins.

By putting in the 5-limit rule, I've made sure that you can't bend my rules. However, this System that starts with maximum coins does not restrict you to 5 plays at any Level. You can now go to 10 plays at any Level, but just for this System.

Notice I did **NOT** release you from Loss Limits, or Naked Pulls and I still hold you to Naked Numbers within this System, but at least you can get a little aggressive by going for 10 plays at the same amount.

The Naked Number is still at 5, which means even though you can string out 10 plays at a Level, you're being checked with a Naked Number amount at 3-4-5-6.

Let's say your Series shows 8 plays at 4 coins and you set 5 as your Naked Number key. If you lose 5 straight pulls at 4 coins each, then you gotta drop to the next lower Level of your predetermined Series, which would be 3 coins. This is a very simple System to understand, even though there is an allowance of several variations and an okay of betting higher amounts to start a Series.

Please, I mean pretty please with chocolate ice cream and whipped cream on it—go back over these paragraphs until you understand Naked Pulls and Naked Numbers.

Let's go to a few examples:

a) 5-5-5-5-5-5-5-4-4-4-4-4-3-3-3-3-2-2-2-5-5-5-5-5-5-5-4-4-4-4-4-3-3-3-3-2-2-2

b) 5-5-5-5-5-5-5-5-3-3-3-3-3-4-4-4-4-4-2-2-2-2-2 (start over)

c) 5-5-5-4-4-4-4-3-3-3-3-3-2-2-2-2-2-2

d) 5-5-5-5-2-2-2-2-5-5-5-5-5-3-3-3-3-5-5-5-5-4-4-4-4

Again I remind you of a tremendous amount of combinations that could be set up, because being able to string out ten plays at every Level gives you an unlimited amount of Series combinations. Just remember these few rules:

a) Series can start at highest coin input.

b) Number of plays at each Level is increased to 10.

c) Loss Limits apply.

d) Naked Pulls apply.

e) Naked Number key is added.

f) If Loss Limits or Naked Pulls are reached, Series is over.

g) If Naked Number is reached, drop to next lowest Level amount.

h) Series is preset ahead of time and never changed.

i) If you reach end of Series and you are still at same machine, start Series over again with same pattern.

This is not a bad System if you have a high enough Session amount. But don't be like the thousands and thousands of players who constantly insist on banging in 5 coins, play after play after play, even though the machine is obviously cold.

That's where Naked Pulls and Naked Numbers moves step in and protect you. Maybe you'll realize that it ain't an act of cowardice to stop putting in maximum coins when the machine is cold.

It's an act of Discipline to have the brains to drop to a lower betting amount until you start winning.

You wanna play this System, do it. But go back and re-read the Theory from the beginning and incorporate all the moves to your play. Start at whatever Level bet you like and work down, and do everything that is called for as to restraints.

This is a method for players with high Bankrolls. There is a tremendous amount of variations of Series to use. The method of using Naked Numbers to drop to a lower betting Level is very efficient.

Go back and re-read this chapter, grasp the Theory, set your Goals and play this system.

It's a good one!

31

Hi-Lo: 3-Coin: System #21

Usually I start explaining a System from the lowest insertion of coins and work up to the max. With the Hi-Lo I started with the maximum 5-coin play and then moved up to an aggressive variation.

To wrap up the System and explain it a litle further, I now give you some plays at the 3-coin machines. But you've probably already laid out your plans.

The basic Theory stays the same, which means you start off betting 3 coins for the amount of plays your Series calls for. There is still a Naked Number set and this could be 3 - 4 - 5 - or 6 losses. The maximum number of plays at any betting Level is 10. In layman's terms that means you can bet 3 coins 120 times in a row. But if you lose 5 in a row (your Named Number, for instance), you gotta drop to the next lowest amount.

This chapter is aimed at those players who wanna use this Theory but play 3-coin machines. Again, there are a ton of possible Series, so pick one of these or come up with your own:

(a) 3-3-3-3-3-2-2-2-2-2-3-3-3-3-3-3-1-1-1-1-1

(b) 3-3-3-3-3-3-3-2-2-2-2-2-1-1-1-1-3-3-3-3-3-3-3-3-2-2-2-2-2-1-1-1-1

(c) 3-3-3-3-3-2-2-2-3-3-3-3-3-2-2-2-3-3-3-3-3-2-2-2

(d) 3-3-3-2-2-2-3-3-3-1-1-1-3-3-3-3-2-2-2-2-1-1-1-1-3-3-3-3-3-
2-2-2-2-2-1-1-1-1-1

Just remember to keep your Series short enough to be able to control your Loss Limits, 'cause you can always go back and start over again. Since you are starting at the maximum coins allowed, there will be times when your Loss Limit will come early.

Remember that the Loss Limit is 60%, or lower if you decide to reduce it. Don't forget that the fraction of an instant that the Loss Limit is reached, your back is to that machine and you're heading for another Session. Don't invest even one more coin.

My friend Watt E. Cey is sitting there with his mouth open, ears clogged, his mind a blank. He thinks this method is too hard to grasp. He thinks all of these systems are a waste of time, an exercise in futility.

He listens with a closed mind to the things I'm trying to teach you. Just take this simple system called the Hi-Lo, at a 3-coin machine. Try to grasp why I am laying out these rules for you.

It is to control every single bet you make, by having you preset how many coins you will play. I am giving you a guide as to when to up your bets, when to lower your bets and when to leave the machine.

What's so wrong about playing with control? This System may not make you rich; in fact, I can't even guarantee that it'll give you a payoff of any size.

But it will control your play, minimize your losses and give you two dynamite things to look for:

1) When you're going bad, lower you bets. If it continues to be bad, leave the machine.

2) When you get ahead with the System, apply the Guarantee and Excess method that will wrap up a guaranteed profit and keep you at a hot machine.

Neither one of these things is even remotely hard to accept. I ain't asking you to kiss your mother-in-law, or hold your breath for 20 minutes, or even tip your paperboy.

I'm asking you to gamble sensibly.

My friend I. M. Madork, with all the wisdom of a dead tree trunk, yet with all the brains he can muster, asks the question still burned into the brains of the dedicated slots player:

"Yeah, you may be right! But I still wanna hit the big jackpot."

I'll never reach him and he'll never hit the big jackpot. But both of us will keep trying. Problem is I just got 8 more gray hairs.

But I'll keep trying!

One more point to this 3-coin Hi-Lo method. You can go as high as 10 plays at any Level but I'd suggest you set your Naked Number at 3.

Three consecutive losses and you drop down to the next lowest betting Level. You also have your Loss Limits and Naked Pulls to protect you.

I like this System a lot. In fact, it's one of my favorites because of the protection it gives you and the added move of dropping my bets to a lower Level when a certain amount of losses in a row occur.

This was a long chapter, but it was used to stress the strong points of a good system.

Trust me!

Incidentally, in case I forgot to say it...when Series ends, go back and start over with same Series.

Stay until you reach Loss Limits or Naked Pulls, or have I said.... Yes I have!

32

Naked Pulls/
Naked Numbers

Let me take a moment to explain the difference between Naked Pulls and Naked Numbers. You know by now that they are both stopgaps that stop you from losing for long periods at any one machine.

The Loss Limits is the mandatory base and then comes additional keys that cut your losses. But you gotta know which is which:

(1) NAKED PULLS: When you start a Session, this is the number you set for consecutive losses to signal your leaving that machine. That number should be between 7 or 14 pulls. You decide which number makes you the most comfortable.

(2) NAKED NUMBER: When you play any system that calls for a long amount of plays at any certain Level, the idea is to reduce the number of pulls at that amount so as not to get hurt. For instance, you have a Series that reads: 3-3-3-3-3-3-3-3-3-3-4-4-4-4-4-4-4-4-4-4-5-5-5-5-5-5-5-5-5-5

You set a Naked number of 4, which means if you are playing four coins at a time and you get 4 empty pulls, you drop down to the next lowest amount and play 3 coins for ten straight pulls. If you had four Naked Pulls at the three-coin insertion, you go down to 2 coins, even though 2 coins was *not* a part of your Series.

Go back over these explanations until you're positive how to use them. You don't gotta be a genius to understand Naked Pulls: that's a certain amount of pulls where you get no returns. Suppose you preset 8 pulls. The instant 8 straight blank pulls is completed, you're gone.

My ex-friend Ed E. Ott asks: "Suppose I'm not pulling the handle, just pressing the button to activate the wheels. Does that count?"

The scary part about this idiot is that he asks that question in all seriousness. Or maybe people like him just like the sound of their own voices asking dumb questions.

With the Naked Number Theory, it is an excellent tool which allows you to stay at a certain machine, but gives you a chance to drop to a lower bet. If you're losing with putting in 4 coins, for example, this gets you to drop to three-coin plays. If you lost 4 times in a row any time during the three-coin play, drop down to two-coin plays.

Just be sure you keep an eye tuned into your Loss Limits and Naked Pulls which signal the end of that Session.

I live and die by the application of Discipline and a conservative approach to gambling. Naked Pulls and Naked Numbers are powerful keys. Please get to understand them, and pretty please use them.

In fact, pretty please with sugar and whipped cream on it.

33

Yo-Yo System:
System #22

You all know what a Yo-Yo is. No, I don't mean Imus Pressit, he has an excuse—he's a nut!

A Yo-Yo is a toy that stretches the limit of its string, all the way as far as it can go, then all the way back to the beginning. It has just two stop points.

This System has the same Theory: all or nothing. Or in simple terms, one coin or five coins. If you're at a three-coin machine, it's one coin or three coins.

My friend Bea Klearer is always asking me to be clearer in explaining my Theories. But even she understands the Yo-Yo. That's because the Theory is so clear. Here are a couple of Series for a 5-coin machine, but it could also be a 3-coin machine:

(a) 1—
(b) 2—
(c) 3—

That's it, that's the whole Series, so don't go looking for the hair on the egg, that's all she wrote.

For instance, you start with one coin. If you lose, stay at one; lose again, stay at one; lose again, stay at one. You win, stretch it up to 5 coins; you win, stay at 5; lose, dive all the way back to one coin.

My friend Kenny Kount can't count to 8 but after weeks of practice he has mastered 1-2-3 (the 3 was giving him trouble). Now I give him a System where he only has to remember 2 numbers (1 and 5). Because that's the only two Levels he will touch.

Kenny Kount is delirious with joy. This yo-yo loves the Yo-Yo and I think you'll see its worth.

If you play at a 3-coin maximum machine, the same Theory would prevail. You'd bet one coin as long as you were losing and jump to 3 coins as soon as you win.

Another win keeps you at 3 coins, while a loss makes you dive to one coin. Simple as 1-2-3. Or in the case of Kenny Kount (who can't count) it's as simple as 1-2.

Now you skeptics are gonna wail that there ain't no Logic to the Yo-Yo. Don't you dare say that, before first grasping the Theory of betting small in bad times and betting high after a win.

I've always remembered a line that Bart Maverick (Jack Kelly) said in one of those Maverick classics.

He was talking to a banker, who asked him if he understood the new-fangled stock market. Maverick gave me a message I've never forgotten, as he said to the banker:

"As my old pappy used to say: Stocks is like poker, bet high when you're winning, bet low when you're losing."

Maverick's pappy did not speak with forked tongue.

34

Should I Play the Slots?

Notice how long I waited before posing this question. It's because that same thought has been banging around in your head every time you pull the handle.

I don't give a rat's tail if you play the Slots or not. But if you do play them, I care *how you bet!*

We're deep into the Money Management Section and it's clear that the true meaning of Money Management is the method you use in making your wagers. There's nothing technical about my Theory, and nothing complicated.

It's all based on what you bet after a win and what you bet after a loss. Plus it all revolves around a system of play that you lay out ahead of time.

When you decide on a Series of bets, you gotta stick with that method until the Session is over. It takes a lot of patience to follow strict Money Management controls but that's the key to winning.

The spinning of the reels in the Slot Machine is the same random process as a pair of dice rolling across a Craps table or a plastic ball bouncing all over a Roulette Wheel.

They are all random situations. It's how you bet that will determine whether you're gonna win or lose. I believe in a conservative style because most people have short Bankrolls.

They'll tell me they go to a casino with a decent Bankroll but the definition of decent is lost on a lot of people.

In the real world, $200 is a lot of money. In the casinos, $200 is a mere pittance. Yet my friend Shorty Shortkash thinks his $100 stake gives him the right to not only play the dollar machines, but put in maximum coins.

This inability to grasp the Reality of his lack of funds will hurt Shorty over and over. One cold run at a dollar machine, with max play, has gotta take its toll and usually does.

So Shorty is not wrong in playing the Slots, he is wrong in his betting methods at those Slots. Yet he is not alone in his stupid approach of betting too high.

Many people come up to me and almost apologize for telling me they are playing the Slots. I tell them they are crazy for assuming I'm gonna mock them. If you're losing at the Slots, it may be time to find a different game. If you're winning at the Slots, I strongly suggest you continue to play them.

Many people play the Slots and that's okeydokey with me. Most of that many play like dorks and that is not acceptable. It's easy to get bored just standing at a machine inserting coins, but that ain't no excuse for blowing money like it didn't matter.

You wanna play the Slots, I ain't gonna condemn you, but if you've come this far in the book, it's obvious you've decided to play seriously. Do this:

(a) Pick a System,

(b) Set up a Series,

(c) Use the Money Management moves,

(d) Accept small wins.

If you do play the Slots, get serious in your approach.

35

Reality

I'm the best player in the casinos. The best, with very few challengers, and I lose 35% of the time. Think about that. I lose about one out of every three days I go to the casinos, and I'm the best. Look at what I go to the casinos with:

(a) A healthy Bankroll,
(b) A complete Knowledge of every game I play,
(c) A strong application of Money Management,
(d) An impeccable handle on Discipline.

That takes care of the Big Four. But go a little further—I also have:

(a) A strong Theory on how to apply my Knowledge and Money Management methods,
(b) A Logical approach to every game and a Logical preset percentage return,
(c) An awareness of Trends and the ability to find and follow them,

Looks like I also go to battle with all the ingredients of the Little 3. That gives me all the things I need to have even a 50-50 chance of winning.

Even with all those things, I'm lucky to scratch out a 15% edge, over and above the 50-50 break-even mark. Well, if I'm so good, why don't I win more than 65% of the time? Because it is so hard to win and I know it, and the scary thing about the

166

reality of all this is that I have everything needed to do battle sensibly, and I still lose almost 35% of the time.

That's the Reality of gambling. It is so important that you grasp the Reality of gambling, that you are subjected to a fourth chapter on Reality.

That's because people like Ed N. Sand sit around with his head in the sand when it comes to gambling.

He thinks that the casinos are places to win thousands of dollars and change his station in life. What a total lack of Reality! The casinos offer you beautiful places to gamble thousands or bet small. But doubling and tripling your money is strictly shooting marshmallows at a tank.

You need too many things to have even a 50-50 shot. You lack one of those seven things I just listed, and your chances of winning take a nose-dive. The reality of it is that only a handful of people have all the ingredients of the Big 4 and Little 3.

But most people don't realize it. Least of all, people like Ed N. Sand.

Most of the time they come to battle lacking 3 or 4 parts of the seven things you need to have. Better they eat dirt than get swallowed at the tables and Slot Machines.

Some of you will learn the Reality of playing conservatively, others will scoff at it, citing you gamble only for fun and not to win money.

Yeah, and politicians make promises they intend to keep.

You wanna get into politics, learn to shovel bull and pass out baloney.

You wanna get into gambling, cut the bull, put away the baloney about playing for fun and accept the reality of it all!

Winning 20% of what you bring to battle makes you a genius. Winning 65% of the time makes you a genius.

Telling me you win double your money most of the time qualifies you for the political field. In other words, you're full of both bull and baloney and oughta run for President.

36

Money Management On Losing Days

The previous chapter explained to you that I lose about 35% of the time, which adds up to a lotta losing days. My goal is to make a day's pay but there are some weeks when I am running good and the returns are quite rewarding.

The key is what to do on losing days and that's where I shine. Since I have known so many losing days, it is imperative that on these days, I must run like a rabbit.

This control on losing days keeps me from putting the family jewels up for ransom. Throughout the book I have screamed at you to leave machines after a certain amount of losses.

There are gonna be days when you lose at 4-5 machines in a row or even 7 out of 10 Slot Sessions right off the bat. That's a scary thing but it'll happen. There's only one way to handle yourself in these cases. That's to reduce those losses. Cut back your Loss Limits, control your Naked Pull limit and stop playing on these days.

I know you don't wanna hear that stuff but it is imperative that you reduce losses on cold days.

Heck, anybody can walk up to a machine, catch a hot run and win a ton of money because the machine gets hot. But how do you handle yourself on losing days?

I've already laid out 38 Systems for you and each of them concentrated on reducing losses. Do you think that was an accident? NO WAY! It was an intentional move to emphasize the importance of holding down losses, because that's so important in the world of gambling.

I've stressed over and over the importance of cutting and reducing losses, yet I'll wager that most of you overlooked that detail. My friend Bette D. House would bet the mortgage if she caught a good machine and would stay at the machine even if it turned cold. She'd say it was due to get hot again.

Bette D. House doesn't have control. She doesn't know how to manage her money on days when she is losing or even on days when she gets ahead, then begins to slip into a cold spell.

It's an art to control losses, especially on days when you're going bad. You're gonna have bad days, losing days, and nothing can change that.

But you can change how you handle yourself on losing days. It's called minimizing losses! Will you grasp this message?

37

Learning How to Win

The previous chapter emphasized holding down losses, while this chapter looks at the other side of the coin. It has to do with winning.

I want you to win at these machines but the problem is that you gotta realize what the term winning is. You gotta get a taste of leaving the casinos with more money than you started with. That's winning.

You gotta sit down and compare winning in the casinos, or in any form of gambling, to how you look at other things that may encompass your thinking:

(a) A ceiling is a few inches over your head. It's called "higher."

(b) You step off the last part of your staircase. It's just a few inches, but you call it "lower."

(c) You spill a quarter of a glass of water on your leg and scream: "I'm soaking wet."

(d) You miss lunch one day. The first thing out of your mouth: "I'm famished—I'm starving to death."

(e) One evening you sneeze because someone put too much pepper on his potatoes: "Oh my God, I'm getting pneumonia."

(f) You pass a good-looking blonde on the street and she happens to glance your way. Your mind explodes: "Holy mackerel, I think she wants me."

(g) You put $1,000 in the bank, get a hefty 4% interest return, and tout yourself as a financial genius, 'cause you made $40 on your investment for a whole year.

Look over all those examples and see if the terms don't coincide with an exaggerated explanation of a happening. Yet when you go to a casino with $200 and win $50, you don't call it "winning," and you don't accept the fact that you have now got more money in your hand than what you started with.

The point is that if you accept the fact that stepping off a staircase, even only seven inches, is considered "down," how can you not call winning $50 with $200 winning? That's a 25% factor.

That's winning, yet a lot of people can't, or won't, accept that 25%, or even anything up to that percentage, as winning. They pour the profits back into the machines. Yet they get a 4% interest check from the bank for a full year's investment and celebrate their newfound bonanza.

These people don't know how to win. They make people like Ed E. Ott look like geniuses.

You gotta "Learn How to Win." You gotta learn to accept small percentage returns. Some day when you do have a gigantic Bankroll, those small percentage returns will look like fortunes.

The same percentage factor prevails. You gotta grasp this Theory, you gotta "Learn How to Win," or have I said that before?

38

Three-Star System: System #23

There are systems in this book for 3-coin machines and 5-coin machines. But let's be serious for a second. Even if you like a system geared for a 5-coin machine, it's a piece of cake to adjust that method to a 3-coin or 2-coin machine.

That adjustment takes place by merely rearranging the Series to comply with the number of coins called for by a certain machine. Same is true if you wanna change a 3-coin Series to a 5-coin or 2-coin machine. Merely adjust the Series by adding or subtracting different Levels.

Each of the Systems I laid out had its own Win Goal, Loss Limit and Naked Pulls. Some also had Naked Numbers applied. All of these things are essential to minimizing losses and taking advantage of Trends.

Sometimes a win calls for a jump to max coins, while other times you were told to just go up to the next Level. On the other side, there were systems that called for a drop to the next Level after a loss and other times you stayed right at the same amount of coin insertions.

In other words, there are a ton of variations, all of them effective but maybe not all of them enticing to you. That's your choice.

What I'd like to do now is go over a couple of systems that re-inforce the power of these moves and give you a method that uses a couple of variations.

The 3-Star System is geared to the 3-coin machine but you can also switch it down to a 2-coin slot or add some Levels for use at a 5-coin slot.

Naturally you gotta set up your Series but by now you oughta be a pro at that because of all the practice you should have put into laying out Series.

The added moves include my favorite move of jumping the bet to a higher Level as soon as a hit occurs. I believe that move should be incorporated into most plays because of the Logical Theory that you wanna take advantage of streaks.

You should also add the "Dip Theory," which calls for a drop to the next lowest Level if you hit your Naked Number designation. Let's say 4 is your Naked Number and 4 blank pulls has you drop a notch to the next lowest betting Level.

With the 3-Star, you use 10 bets per Level, have a $30 Session amount for fifty-cent machines and a $20 Session amount for quarter machines.

If you're gonna play dollar slots, I want $50 per Session. If that irritates you, then you ain't grasped a doggone ounce of Theory regarding the importance of proper Bankroll.

Here are some examples:

a) 1-1-1-1-1-1-1-1-1-1-2-2-2-2-2-2-2-2-2-2-3-3-3-3-3-3-3-3-
3-3-2-2-2-2-2-2-2-2-2-2-3-3-3-3-3-3-3-3-3-3-1-1-1-1-1-1-1-1-1-1

Then start over:

(b) 2-2-2-2-2-2-2-2-2-2-1-1-1-1-1-1-1-1-1-1-2-2-2-2-2-2-2-2-2-3-
3-3-3-3-3-3-3-3-3-2-2-2-2-2-2-2-2-2-2-1-1-1-1-1-1-1-1-1-1-
2-2-2-2-2-2-2-2-2-3-3-3-3-3-3-3-3-3-3

(c) 3-3-3-3-3-3-3-3-3-3-2-2-2-2-2-2-2-2-2-2-1-1-1-1-1-1-1-1-1-1-
3-3-3-3-3-3-3-3-3-3-2-2-2-2-2-2-2-2-2-2-1-1-1-1-1-1-1-1-1-1

Just to go over this method, I like the fact that there are 10 plays at each level, with the protection coming from the Naked Number addition. Let's say the Naked Number you set is 4 and the Naked Pulls is 9.

(1) If you have 9 Naked Pulls, the Session is over, so you're protected against a disaster.

(2) If you have 4 Naked Numbers in a row, you drop to next lowest Level, cutting down a heavy insertion of coins at a high Level on a cold machine.

(3) Jumping a notch to a higher Level after a win ensures your catching a nice return if machine stays hot.

With the 3-Star System you have an option move when you jump a Level after a win.

(a) Stay at the Level you jumped to and complete that line,

(b) If Loss occurs when you jumped to next highest Level after a win, slide back to the Level you jumped from.

If you want my opinion, I'd stay with:

(a) That keeps you at a higher play, to complete that line and then pick up the Series you predetermined.

Since there are only three size bets (one-coin, two-coin, or three-coin), this was an easy decision. But you decide what option you like.

This was a rather long chapter, but a very important one because of its use of so many moves. You may wanna take a second look at the 3-Star.

You may wanna use it the way I laid it out, or you may wanna add a twist or two.

I like the 3-Star and think you will too.

39

Five-Star System: System #24

The 3-Star System is very easy to understand, due to the fact that you should have a strong grasp of my Theories by now. Along those same lines, the 5-Star System is merely a jump to a higher coin insertion, with the same application of all the 3-Star moves, plus any variations you may have added.

But as simple as I make it, there's my friend Ken U. Bulleve over there scratching his head. Can you believe that Ken U. Bulleve does not believe in applying systems to Slots, even though I've explained to him over and over, the need of Discipline for any form of gambling?

For you other people, who still believe that Systems and Money Management should only be applied to the table games, you're all wet.

If you're gonna play Slots, you better believe you better use Money Management, regardless of whether Ken U. Bulleve doesn't believe you should believe me or whether he does believe you believe me.

I can't believe I just wrote that sentence. There is a message there that you better believe in, or believe me you better not waste your time playing Slots if you don't believe me.

Anyhow, let's get to the 5-Star System.

The same added moves of Naked Numbers should be used, along with the upping and dipping of bets, as was explained in the 3-Star System chapter.

One thing I wanna stress in this chapter is the use of longer plays at each level, as long as you have the proper Session amount.

This will allow you to increase your Naked Number to 5 or 6 and give you the play of a double dip to the second lowest Level after your Naked Number is activated. Either a full jump to maximum coins after a win, or just a jump to the next Level after a win is an option that you can choose.

Let's start with a jump of one Level after a win, as explained in the 3-Star System. You can stay with that play and stay at that Level for the completion of the line or you can come back to the Level you were at when you got the win. You already know all that, but decide what you want to do.

Let me give you another option. Suppose you're at the 2-coin line and get 3 bars. You jump to the 3-coin line and get 2 cherries. Now you jump to the 4-coin line and 3 bars show again. You go up to the 5-coin Level.

You keep going up a Level after every score. When a loss occurs, you either finish out that line, or dip all the way back to the 2-coin insertions where the win started. You don't have to have a doctor's degree in mathematics to understand this, but you should concentrate on what moves you predetermined to use before the Series started.

I'll lay out a couple of Series and then we'll cover the moves from the losing side (all 20 play lines):

(a) 3-3-3-3-3-3-3-3-3-3-3-3-3-3-3-3-3-3-3-3-3-1-1-1-1-1-1-1-1-1-1-1-1-1-1-1-1-1-1-1-4-4-4-4-4-4-4-4-4-4-4-4-4-4-4-4-4-4-4-4-2-2-2-2-2-2-2-2-2-2-2-2-2-2-2-2-2-2-2-2-5-5-5-5-5-5-5-5-5-5-5-5-5-5-5-5-5-5-5-5

(b) 4-4-4-4-4-4-4-4-4-4-4-4-4-4-4-4-4-4-4-4-1-1-1-1-1-1-1-1-1-1-1-1-1-1-1-1-1-1-1-1-3-3-3-3-3-3-3-3-3-3-3-3-3-3-3-3-3-3-3-3-2-2-2-2-2-2-2-2-2-2-2-2-2-2-2-2-2-2-2-2-5-5-5-5-5-5-5-5-5-5-5-5-5-5-5-5-5-5-5-5

Notice I left the max bet last in both of those Series, 'cause I want you to be able to jump to the highest play, if that is the option you use. Also, with a small or modest Bankroll, you wanna play as conservatively as possible, in the event of a cold machine when you first start playing.

With the use of the jump method, of going up after a hit, you get to play max coins very often, but only when that machine is hitting.

Suppose you play the 5-Star method with Series (b) which I just laid out. You could set your Naked Pull at 10 and your Naked Number at 5.

Let's say you're on the first line and the machine started off cold. You quickly pick up five losing pulls in a row, so your Naked Number has come up. You have three options:

(1) Drop one Level to playing 3 coins and finish out the line,

(2) Double Dip to the 2-coin line and finish out the plays,

(3) Dive all the way to the one-coin line and play at this lowest Level until a score comes.

With a score you have two options:

(a) Go up one Level with the win,

(b) Leap all the way to max coin play.

This 5-Star System has a ton of options, using all of the plays that I've given you. It turns playing the slots into an experience of Discipline, Money Management and optional patterns.

I would take (b): Leap all the way to 5-coin max play. Stay there if you continue to win. Double Dip after a loss.

You either play this way or lay out the moves where you feel most comfortable.

Notice how the Systems in this book started slowly, then gradually worked up to the ultimate multiple-choice 3-Star and 5-Star System? That's because there are so many ways for you to play slots with a strong preset approach.

Digest this System: Please.

40

Guarantee and Excess Again!

Read this chapter! Yeah, you've heard me say that before but not too many times. In fact, the only time I said it was in the chapters that emphasize Loss Limits and cutting your chances of losing. Look back at Chapter 15 in this section. Same Theory is repeated.

Again I swing over to the winning part of your play and show you how to handle those days. It all comes down to a move I call Guarantee and Excess.

I asked my friend Noah Little, who knows a little about everything, or so he says, and he was happy to expound his words of wisdom. I asked him what Guarantee and Excess meant.

"Well, uh, that you gotta have, uh, a Guarantee and a, well, man, you gotta have X's."

"Sit down, Mr. Noah Little!"

Guarantee and Excess means exactly what it sounds like. It is a move you make after your Win Goal is reached. You wanna set up the Guarantee and Excess move:

(a) Take your Win Goal and break it in half.

(b) Put your Session amount in your pocket.

(c) Put half of the Win Goal in your pocket; that's called

Guarantee.

(d) The other half of the Win Goal is kept on the table, called your Excess.

(e) You continue to play at that table as long as your Excess is alive.

I've gone over this before, but isn't that a beautiful exercise? Can you honestly see the Logic of taking your Win Goal and locking up a profit?

Remember that percentage story where I explained that "70% of the people who enter a casino get ahead and 90% of that 70% give it back?"

Well, the Guarantee and Excess move protects you. First you lock up a profit and then you get the opportunity to stay at that session or machine and take advantage of the obvious hot pattern.

This was all explained earlier in the book but the importance of the move warrants a second explanation.

Like it or not, the next two chapters again delve deeper into the Theory, so if you wanna skip them, that's okay with me.

But if you have any one of the following characteristics, you must read those chapters:

(1) You qualify for the human race by being alive.

(2) You can count to three by ones.

(3) You know where to put the coin in the slot machine.

Anybody who does have at least one of these three things must read these chapters.

I realize this disqualifies my buddies, Imus Pressit, Ed E. Ott and I. M. Madork, but since the only thing they qualify for is a charter membership in the first order of dorks, I doubt if they would even understand what I'm saying anyhow.

You others... read these chapters.

This is the second time I covered this Theory because of its colossal importance.

41

Excess Excellence

Now we swing over to the handling of the Excess, the amount of money you can invest into that same machine with two different options:

   (a) Continue with the same system that got you your Win Goal.

   (b) Become aggressive, because you realize you have a profit socked away and no way you can lose at this Session.

Either one of these two choices is acceptable and actually it comes to the make-up of each individual player. You'll know yourself how you wish to handle that Excess and it is not my intent to lead you in any specific direction.

There is merit to using (a) where you dance with the gal you brung to the hop. Why change a good thing?

There is merit to using (b) where you got the chance to go for the biggie, 'cause you can't lose at that Session, so why not go for the Queen of the Ball? My suggestion would be—Oh, you don't wanna hear my suggestion, this is one of those times you should make your own choice.

But there is something you absolutely must do when you reach the Excess point of your Win Goal.

MANDATORY: You must pay yourself for every single solitary subsequent winning pull, and if you were paying attention, I also told you this a few chapters back.

It merely means that once you reach the Excess stage, I want you to pay yourself for every winning pull. That means that even if you get three coins with a single quarter bet, when 2 cherries appear, you gotta put at least one quarter with the Guarantee. If you win 14 coins, then I'd like you to put 50% of them with the Guarantee.

In other words, I'd like you to put 50% of whatever you win with the Guarantee, but you decide how you wanna divide it. My suggestion is 50%, but most of all I want something put aside.

In simple terms, just remember this sentence whenever you have any doubts:

"When you reach the excess part of your Win Goal, every subsequent profit should be broken in half: One half with the Guarantee, the other half stays with the Excess."

Even that demon of dense, Watt E. Cey, who has trouble understanding the first three sentences we got in school:

(1) See Spot.

(2) See Spot run.

(3) See Spot run fast.

Watt E. Cey was in the seventh grade when he discovered the subject was a dog. He thought it was a gushy spot on his mother's rug.

But even though he has little sense, he understands dollars. He can see putting aside one when he has two in his hand.

That's what I want you to see. The power of splitting profits in half has a twofold purpose:

(1) It increases the Guaranteed money you'll leave the machine with,

(2) It increases the Excess, the money you can keep playing with.

If you follow the rules of Guarantee and Excess, you'll get those days where a machine eventually explodes with a big payout. Even if it doesn't, you already have your profit locked away.

One final thought. When you're playing with your Excess, you are still controlled by Naked Pulls, although I will allow you to stretch them a little further than 15. How about 16?

But don't blow the whole Excess back. If you see the machine is cold, grab what's left, stash it with your Guarantee and leave that machine a happy cat!

Reread these last two chapters.

Then go back and reread chapters 18 and 19 in this section. Same church, different pew!

42

Excess Power Move

I think I told you this story but forget if it was in this book or if it came up at a Seminar.

Anyhow, it's good enough to repeat and for my friend Rhee Repeet, you can't repeat things enough times.

But since I'm going a little senile anyhow, you gotta expect the mind to lapse into periods of forgetfulness. In fact, I already forgot what I was gonna tell you, 'cause I couldn't remember if I told you or not.

That's why I never get mad at my friend Ivor Gott, because of his lapses into forgetfulitis.

But I won't tolerate the rest of you forgetting the moves that are laid out for you. They will sometimes seem stupid or too conservative for your previous style, but after you get into consistent wins, you'll swing over to my style and that's when you'll remember my words of a few chapters ago: "Learn How to Win."

Along these lines, let me give you this system that I saw my mother using. She is very conservative playing the Slots and loves the idea of winning, regardless of the amounts.

One day I walked over to where she was playing a machine and obviously she had a good hot run. She had already reached her Win Goal and broken the profits in half.

She had a bucket that contained her Session money and

Guarantee at her feet and the other bucket was half full of quarters. It was her Excess.

She was playing from this Excess bucket, but it was a little wrinkle she was using that caught my eye.,

Her series was laid out in a 2-2-2-2-2-3-3-3-3-3-2-2-2-2-2-3-3-3-3-3 pattern. She was at a three-coin machine and did not use any plays at one coin during the Series.

When I got there, she was playing 3 coins at a time. She got 3 bars and was paid 30 coins. She put 15 of them into the Guarantee bucket.

She lost the next pull and put 3 coins in the Guarantee bucket. Again she lost and put 3 coins in the Guarantee pail. Then came 2 cherries, a profit of 9 coins, and she rat-holed 5 of them.

Three losses followed and each time she dropped 3 coins into the Guarantee. Did you notice the pattern? She was putting half her profits with the Guarantee but she was also paying herself 3 coins on the pulls that resulted in no return.

I loved the move and asked her where she came up with the idea. She said: "I didn't like the idea of not getting a return on every pull, so every play gives me a profit."

I asked her what she'd do if she was playing one coin at a time. "Same idea. I put half my winnings with the Guarantee and one coin with the Excess. Even with a loss."

I really loved the idea and had absolutely nothing to do with its origination. But look at the Theory: You're paying yourself when you win and paying yourself when you lose.

Let's go a little deeper, but maybe some of you already thought of it. My mother was using this method *after* she reached her Win Goal.

What's so wrong with using the same method all the time? In other words, even the start of a Session has you popping a coin into the Guarantee bucket right from the get-go.

A cold machine will naturally hurt you and even with the Loss Limit and Naked Pulls to protect you, this little extra move is a nice twist.

Give it some thought and give it a try. The amount you rat-hole after a loss is your choice, but at least drop one coin into that Guarantee bucket. It's that much fewer coins you can lose.

I always offer $10,000 to anyone who gives me a system that I think worthy of passing along in my books and videos, but I don't think she knows about that offer and I certainly won't tell her.

She usually buys all my books (I give her a dollar off, 'cause after all she is my mother), but I'll tell her this book sells for $620 and maybe she won't buy it, so I'll save the $10,000.

But I do like the approach and recommend it highly.

Think about it. It's got a lot of merit.

43

The Last System:
System #25

I've saved the easiest System for last because even though all of you people wanna win, only about 30% of you believe you should have a Money Management method for playing Slots.

Of that 30%, only about a dozen of you will actually follow these strict money controlled methods. That's because you really haven't grasped the true reality of gambling and how tough it is to win.

My friend Don Beeleave doesn't believe anything I say about Money Management can help him at the Slots. After reading all the Systems, his reasons for not following them include:

(a) Too time consuming.

(b) Too much trouble.

(c) It gives him a headache trying to remember the systems.

(d) Prevents him from winning jackpots most of the time. (He hasn't won one yet in 23 years of playing Slots.)

(e) Doesn't like moving to different machines so much.

(f) Believes you should only play max coins all the time, even if your Bankroll is only $30.

(g) Doesn't know why he doesn't like the approach, can't think of a good reason to knock it, but knocks it anyhow, just on principle.

Maybe you don't believe in Systems, just like Don Beeleave, but you'd better realize that the only way you're gonna grind out consistent returns, is by controlling your money and reducing losses. But enough of that, here's the final System and we'll call it "Simple System." (That's pretty original.)

We'll say you have a small Bankroll, perhaps $100, and wanna spend the day in the casino. You accept the fact that you have a small Bankroll, and you accept the fact that you'll accept a nice 30% or 40% return on your Session money. I'll accept that acceptance because it's intelligent.

Set your Naked Pulls, we'll say 9, and your Loss Limits and Win Goals at 60%. You'll take $5 to the machine, which is 20 quarters.

It doesn't matter if you go to a 3-coin or a 5-coin machine. You'll always start with the middle bet. That merely means that a 3-coin machine starts with a 2-coin bet and the 5-coin machine begins with 3 coins.

Here's how simple it is. We'll assume you're at a 5-coin machine but it could be a 3-coin, as the Theory is identical.

(a) Insert 3 coins.

(b) If you win on first pull, jump to max coins.

(c) Stay at max coins as long as you keep getting winning pulls.

(d) As soon as a loss occurs, you drop one Level.

(e) Each time you win, you always jump to max coins.

(f) A loss calls for a drop of one Level.

(g) Once you get to one coin, you stay there if you keep losing.

(h) You play until you lose 9 in a row, or whatever your Naked Pull is.

(i) There is no Naked Number for this System, only Naked Pulls and Loss Limits.

(j) Loss Limit is 60%. In the case of $5 Session amount, this is $3.

(k) You go to max coins after a win and stay there as you win, and drop a Level at each loss.

How can you get a simpler System than the Simple System? You're betting max coins when winning and dropping a Level at each loss. You can't lose more than 60% of your starting Session amount and the Naked Pulls is a back-up protection valve.

This is for all you people with short Bankrolls. I gave you $5 per Session, but you can make it $10 and reduce your Loss Limit to 40% or 50% if you'd like.

If your Session amounts are higher and you wanna play at 50¢ or dollar machines, use the same Theory. Just make sure you have the proper Bankroll.

That means a dollar machine calls for at least $30 per Session. The 50¢ machine calls for at least $15 per Session. I really like the Simple System because it is restrictive, in that you can't get hurt bad. Then again it keeps you into accepting a 60% return and then reverting to the use of the Guarantee and Excess.

Try the Simple System!

44

Finalizing Systems

This is one final look at Systems and just wanna elaborate on a couple of the most important things that you should concentrate on.

My ex-friend Phil O. Krapps is a constant thorn in my side. He continues to berate me for insisting that people should accept small returns and utilize Money Management at every turn.

He ridicules the use of Discipline and all other controls that I maintain is important to winning in the casinos. Phil O. Krapp is full of crap when it comes to gambling intelligence.

I can't give you a System that works all the time, 'cause there ain't none. I can't give you Systems that guarantee a 30% return every trip to the Slots, 'cause there ain't none, and I can't make you rich with gambling 'cause your chances of winning 20% of your Bankroll is only 50-50.

So how can you expect to win thousands with hundreds? You can't, at least not the majority of times.

But I can teach you how to cut losses, save money, play logically and accept small percentage returns:

These are the things to zero in on:

(a) Pick out 5 or 6 of the Systems I gave you and master them.

(b) Play within the confines of your Bankroll.

(c) Don't deviate from the System you decide upon at a

certain machine.

(d) Set Naked Pulls.

(e) Set Naked Numbers.

(f) If use Dip Method or Dive Method, be sure you stay consistent.

(g) If you play Hi-Lo, be sure you decide on how high you jump (one Level or to Max coins).

(h) Predetermine if you'll stay at max coins or return to existing Level bet after a loss.

(i) Be sure you lay out your Series before you play and follow it to the T.

(j) Don't be afraid to write your Series out and glance at it while you're playing.

(k) Absolutely set your Win Goals at each machine.

(l) When reach Win Goal, utilize Guarantee and Excess.

(m) Most of all, above all, above everything else, even more important than returning a call from Racquel Welch, or for you ladies Paul Newman, set your Loss Limits.

(n) Finally, be sure you set Loss Limits, or have I said that already?

That in a nutshell is your guide to handling a Session (machine). I know it's gonna be tough. I know you won't follow all the rules. You'll say it's too hard, just to win a few dollars.

No, it ain't too tough. It's like taking medicine that's good for you. The first impulse is to pooh-pooh controls. Well, taking medicine is good for you and following these controlled rules is good for you.

Of the thousands of people who will read this book, maybe 2% will follow all the rules. The rest will be moaning about their bad luck and how God makes you lose 'cause he hates you.

What a crock of crap. You lose because you lack the guts to use Money Management consistently. Will you change and follow the rules?

Don't be sil, you'd rather lose and have something to moan about.

What a pity!

Discipline

1

What Is Discipline?

Yeah, yeah, you're gonna tell me you know all about Discipline. You're gonna tell me you should have Discipline if you expect to win in the casino. You're gonna tell me you got a Bankroll, you know the games, and you know how to bet.

Then you'll say, "Gee, the only thing I lack is a little Discipline." Hey baby, you're lacking the brakes that stop the car. Talking about lacking Discipline is like jumping out of a plane without a parachute, then saying: "Gee, I wish I remembered to bring along a chute."

Having 3 parts of the Big 4 ain't nearly enough. Each has its own important input that allows you to get ahead, but when you reach a point where you get a profit socked away, you gotta have the guts to follow your predetermined move, and that's to quit a winner.

It doesn't necessarily have to be quitting a table with a 10% profit, but at least you gotta use my Theory of Guarantee and Excess. That allows you to rat-hole a profit but continue to play.

191

It takes a lot of Discipline to leave a table with a 10% profit, even if that profit is only 10%. It doesn't take much brains to get ahead and give "your" profit back to the house.

Discipline is really a gutsy move. It's control over your basic intent to go for the big kill. Sure, you wanna win thousands. We all do! But it rarely is gonna happen, no matter how hard you wish you could get lucky and win a fortune.

Don't forget, Discipline is not just quitting with a profit, it's also quitting when you're going bad and the streaks are all going against you.

In fact, it's easier to quit when you're winning than being able to quit when you're losing. Yet it is even more important that you set these limits on your losses, so as not to fall so deep in debt, that 15 winning days, with small returns, won't even help you.

Discipline is control. It's setting stopgaps in losses and intelligent realistic goals on the win side. But it's tough to follow these controls once you're inside the casino and the hustle and bustle of casino life engulfs you.

Discipline is hard to acquire and even harder to maintain. You'll know you're lacking it if you've been consistently coming home from the casino broke, even though most of those times you were ahead a few bucks.

You'll skim through this section, nodding that I'm right, then going out and playing like a dork.

If you don't got Discipline, or refuse to apply it to your play, gambling ain't for you.

2

Steps of Discipline

I hope you've given some thought to toning down your crazy approach to the slots and consider setting some controls:

Let me lay out some things you should do, which constitute Discipline:

    (a) Go to the casino when you've accumulated a decent Bankroll.

    (b) Take the time to select a System you're comfortable with.

    (c) Study the System until you're perfectly sure you understand it.

    (d) Break Bankroll into Sessions, even though you might dislike being controlled.

    (e) Leave the machine the exact instant you hit your Loss Limit.

    (f) Leave the machine the exact instant you hit your Naked Pulls.

    (g) Take the time to break your Win Goal into Guarantee and Excess.

    (h) If you get ahead and start to lose, be sure you bring a profit away from that machine.

Each of these points lead to helping you cut losses and take advantage of Trends. You can be sure I'm aware that you're used to the fast pace of Slot playing.

It's an exercise in perpetual motion and my suggestions will cut into that fast pace. But it'll make you a Disciplined player and that has to improve your chances of winning.

Will you listen? Will you try these few little steps I give you? Maybe some of you will give it a shot, but the fraction of an instant that someone questions what you're doing, you'll panic. You'll feel intimidated because it'll look like you're using a system at the machines and so far that's unheard of at Slots. You'll try to hide the paper with the System.

You'll panic and mutter something about the fact that you're not playing a System but merely checking out certain pieces of paper so you can deposit your gum into a clean piece of white paper.

Then you'll slide back into your previous helter-skelter method of play. Far be it from you to have someone think you're using Discipline and a controlled method of play.

Yeah, you want Discipline and you know you need it, but you won't even take a second look at those few steps I laid out for you.

Tsk! Tsk! Tsk!

3

The Last Coin

Here's a message that's gonna be aimed at and hit most of you. We've all been guilty of this massive display of stupidity. It has to do with betting down to the last coin. What idiotic reasons are behind people making this move? Listen to these statements:

(1) Hey, it could be the start of a scorching run.

(2) Hey, it's just another coin.

(3) I didn't feel like putting it back in my pocket.

(4) It's only a quarter.

These reasons were not given by a group of four-year-olds, although the analogy makes it sound like it was uttered by:

(a) A room of idiots,

(b) A couple of kids who failed kindergarten,

(c) A tree full of monkeys.

No, they were given by people with less intelligence than the three examples previously mentioned. They were uttered by Slots players.

Yeah, they sound so stupid when you jot them down on a piece of paper, yet you'll get that type of reasoning day after day.

For just this reason, I gave you Naked Pulls and Naked Numbers and Loss Limits. It puts a stop on losses and restricts you from pouring too many coins into a cold machine.

But even for the thousands of people who won't accept my

Naked Pulls and Loss Limits, don't fall into the trap of betting down to your last few coins.

I see people at the table games falling prey to this move.

They buy in at a Blackjack table with $100 and bet right down to that last chip. Do they really think that last chip is gonna recoup all those previous 19 lost chips? Don't be sil.

Remember that old commercial about a coffee that was good right to the last drop? I can buy that.

But your chances of winning back all your losses ain't a good move down there at that last chip. Save the money to get yourself a hot cup of coffee. It'll do you more good than the fairy tale you think is gonna be sprung with your final play.

Give this message a second thought. Zero in on the Loss Limits I advise. What a gigantic turnabout you'll be in for if you can cut your losses—and this is one of the places to start!

4

The Author and Discipline

The reason I know so much about Money Management and Discipline is because all the bad habits you now have were invented by me years ago.

I broke every rule of Discipline and some that still weren't invented. There was no logic to my play and no direction. It was a helter-skelter exercise in stupidity.

Back in the sixties, I played the Slots daily in Las Vegas. At that time the casinos used real silver dollars. The returns were about 92% and since there weren't that many casinos or that many players, the casinos would do anything to get the business.

Loose slots were a big draw. I'd head back to my motel room at 4 A.M., dragging my feet, 'cause my pants were weighed down by batches of silver dollars.

If I had any brains, I'd have stored away all those silver dollars, sent them home and waited till the 1970s when you got double and triple value for those silver coins.

But all I did was re-invest the coins and everything else I could find into a Poker game, a Craps game, or sure-fire sporting event, where it was impossible to lose. Or so I thought.

The fact that I always got ahead and always poured the money back, is genuine proof that I was the biggest dork in Vegas.

Sandy Koufax, one of the greatest pitchers of all time, had

trouble losing a ball game—unless I happened to be betting on him to win.

I wouldn't bet to win necessarily. I just wanted the action. There were days I'd be playing at a downtown casino, standing between a Roulette table and a Blackjack table.

I'd have bets on both games, playing a dozen numbers straight up at the Roulette table and two or three hands at the Blackjack table—at the same time.

In one hand was a Keno ticket, which I kept playing all day long.

They flashed the numbers on monitors all over the casino. In my back pocket was a list of ball games I had bets on, and every fifteen minutes I checked the scores to see if I was winning or losing a certain contest.

There was no such thing as Win Goals, Loss Limits or Discipline. I kept betting with both hands, in a non-stop excursion to nowhere.

If I won a lot of money that day, I'd get into a high-stakes Poker game that night. If I lost a lot of money that day, I'd get into a low-stakes Poker game that night. I was a dork.

The only thing that saved me was that some smart old-timer, who knew what gambling was about, buttonholed me and steered me in the right direction. He told me all about Discipline and smart playing.

I'm trying to pass this info over to you. You're gonna either accept it or reject it. A lot of you will grasp what I'm saying. A lot of you will say you're in complete control. You'll get 3 sevens on a hot Slots, get ahead $1,000 and scream your joy to anyone who'll listen.

The next day in the office you'll be telling the war stories to your buddies, how $1,000 was just your steppingstone to a really big day.

You'll tell them that even though you blew the $1,000 back, you had a ball.

That's the exact same stories I told in those days when I thought I was so smart. I wasn't!

5

Smart Percentage Return

Here's another chapter you ain't gonna like, so you might wanna skip it. I realize that a lot of you ain't gonna wanna hear about Discipline, so when you get to chapters that restrict your play, you find ways to close your mind to the message.

Well, get skipping, 'cause this chapter is gonna tell you to adjust your thinking down to a realistic percentage return.

All book long I've been telling you to set 60% Loss Limits. That's to get you tuned into setting goals.

Well, I've been lying to you. The goal of 60% is a tad high. I give you that amount so you can be excited about the prospects of getting that good a return. Then when you're all settled into setting goals, I sneak in the back door and tell you to re-think your thinking.

How about 50%, or even 40%. It'd be a lot easier to reach a goal of 40% and wouldn't it be nice to head home from the casinos with more money than what you brought? Of course it'd feel great, but then again some of you never get to have that feeling.

I'm gonna show you a table, based on what I look for as a return at the tables. Remember, it's based on a higher Bankroll, but the Theory is what I'm trying to get you to zero in on. The more you bring, the lesser percentage you shoot for:

BANKROLL	PERCENTAGE RETURN
$ 200	30%
$ 500	20%
$ 700	15%
$1,000	10%
$2,000	8%
$5,000	6%

No, you ain't gonna agree with this Theory at first glance. But you will eventually see its power as you get more involved in gambling.

The Logical reasoning will become evident as soon as you realize how tough it is to win. Don't forget, the Win Goal does not demand you quit for the day. It shows you how to rat-hole a profit by using the Guarantee and Excess. Then you can take a real shot with the Excess.

Since it's easier to win 10% then it is to win 60%, why not try for the smaller percentage return until you get in the habit of winning consistently, regardless of the amount.

I realize a lot of you got small Bankrolls, so all the more reason for you to accept smaller returns.

My friend Count U. Muny, a real life count, brings a big Bankroll to the tables and can bet crazy. But you do not have Count U. Muny's money, so I want you to re-evaluate your money situation and react accordingly.

That means you count your money as you enter the casino and set a nice small Win Goal, which should be easy to reach.

You'll get in the habit of winning and you will love it. The days of big returns are rare, but someday you'll have the Bankroll to go for the kill.

Just have patience, my friends. Patience!

6

Discipline on Losing Days

I lose a lot in the casinos, maybe 30% to 35% of the time. Yet I'm a great player, because at the end of the year I have a profit. The reasons are simple:

(a) I accept small returns, so I quit with small profits, giving me a lot of winning days, even though my wins may be small dollar amounts.

(b) I cut my losses on losing days by quitting before I get wiped out.

Both of these moves are important. That's why I've harped so much about Naked Pulls, Naked Numbers and Loss Limits, chapter after chapter. It's so imperative that you cut your losses on those days when things ain't going good. The temptation is to keep banging away, figuring that things will change.

It don't take brains to analyze the things we do: I have quirks:

(1) I eat because I'm hungry.

(2) I drink because I'm thirsty.

(3) I gamble because I want money.

(4) I use Discipline because I hate to lose.

(5) I play sports because I'm good.

(6) I don't dance because I can't.

(7) I eat candy because I have lapses in Discipline.

(8) I don't sing because I'm lousy.

(9) I think of Sophia Loren because I'm in love.

All of the above are desires or acts that take Discipline. (All except (9), that's just a waste of time.)

But it doesn't bother me to have chinks in my armor, as long as they are controlled. You're gonna have days when you're losing and you'll let your losses get out of control.

These things happen and that you can't fight. But as long as the lapses in Discipline are corrected, you'll have a good shot in the casinos.

Handling yourself on days you are losing is gonna be tough. But it's mandatory you realize you're gonna lose on certain days and you steel yourself to curtail those losses.

You'll have days when everything is going right and whatever you do turns into a plus. Just have the Discipline to control the losses on the bad days.

7

The Loudmouth

The Loudmouth is no stranger to the casinos. You see them at the Craps table, the Blackjack table or wherever a crowd seems to gather and gamble.

If you don't see him, it's for sure you'll hear him. He has a knack for drawing attention to himself, if for no other reason than to feed an ego that needs constant refueling.

The Loudmouth ain't just loud. He's also got a mixture of . boring, irritable and pesty attributes all mixed in with his personality. Funny thing is, he always happens to be at the machine next to you.

When he's winning, he shouts to the world that he's blessed with a certain gift that allows him to zero in on hot machines.

While he's in that winning streak he's all hoot and holler. He offers advice to people at all neighboring machines, oblivious to the fact that they might be in a losing Trend and not too receptive to his childish prattles.

But the Loudmouth doesn't slow down. He chastises some little old lady for playing only one quarter and occasionally will flip her a couple of coins, then proclaim it to the world how generous he is: "Hey, little lady, here's a few chips from old Buck to get you started on your second million. Guess you're glad you were lucky enough to play in my aisle."

Then he laughs at his own words and waits for nods of

approval from the other players for his show of generosity.

This pompous boor is too wrapped up in his own self-importance to see the glances of disgust from the other players.

When a cocktail waitress goes by, he reaches out to stop her and proceeds to make snide remarks about her costume and physical attributes.

His off-color remarks are said loud enough to try and provoke giggles from the other players, but he's too dumb to see their disgust.

His obnoxious behavior continues as long as he's winning. But the instant this Loudmouth slips into a losing spell, his whole manner changes.

He curses his luck, sneers at the other players and threatens bodily harm to any little old lady who may happen to take a machine near him.

The cocktail waitress he was so forward with is now subjected to his vile comments and he insults her because there were only 3 ice cubes in his free drink instead of 4 or 5, and his drink was too warm.

He screams about fixed machines, cheating casinos and anything else that comes to his infant mind. The Loudmouth makes it uncomfortable for anyone unlucky enough to happen by.

His whole outlook is keyed on what is happening to *him* and everyone else be hanged. And the Loudmouth always seems to find the aisle you're playing in.

You can't hide from these jerks and there's no use trying to reason with them. They're in every casino, at every game and they seem to multiply like mosquitoes.

The Slot hosts recognize the type and avoid them. The casinos tolerate these Loudmouths and try not to encourage their returning to that particular establishment.

There's nothing you can do about changing these dorks or trying to discourage them. They're a disease that sickens everyone who comes in contact with them.

The players all hate him, the hosts avoid him, the casino

personnel hope this jerk drowns himself in his own pool of obnoxiousness. The Loudmouth brings his own bag of cement.

8

The Professional Gambler

I've written eight other books on gambling and they're listed toward the end of the next section. In each book I discuss the things you need to win, but also try to give you insight into all parts of gambling.

In my *Advanced Craps* book I wrote a chapter about the Professional Gambler who gives you a look at that life. Instead of writing a new chapter, I just put that one in this section. Maybe it'll give you a sneak look into the pro's outlook.

You don't have to be Fred Astaire to dance, you don't have to be Larry Bird to play basketball, you don't have to be Frank Sinatra to sing, you don't have to be a kid to like Christmas, you don't have to be Irish to wear green, but you gotta be good to win at gambling.

So despite the millions and millions of people who gamble, only a handful can make a living at it. They are professional gamblers.

I ain't trying to say you should be a professional gambler but at least you should use the Discipline that they exhibit.

After all, you use your feet like Fred Astaire, your shooting hand like Larry Bird, your voice like Frank Sinatra, you approach Christmas with the same outlook as a kid and you even lie about your Irish vintage. (Believe it or not, I'm writing this chapter on March 17th and so far today I was greeted by several guys decked in green from head to foot. Their names were Tony, Nick, Angelo and Roberto.)

So why is it when you gamble, you emulate one of the seven dwarfs? (Dopey!)

I've been gambling since bread was 11¢ a loaf and I know how to lose. In fact, I was so dumb that it was the only thing I was good at.

My gut feeling about gambling was that everybody lost. I was living proof that a fool and his money are soon parted.

There were weeks when I'd win on Monday, Tuesday and Wednesday, be broke on Thursday, pull ahead Friday and Saturday and give it all back on Sunday.

My initial trips to Vegas allowed me to come in contact with guys who made a living gambling. These pros played at the tables where I dealt when I was broke, which was most of the time.

They didn't win all the time but their losses were small.

They played Poker like rocks, Blackjack with impeccable decisions and Craps with unbelievable control. From them I learned how to win. I think the biggest thing these pros showed me was that smart gamblers weren't always the High Rollers.

Somewhere in the back of my mind I always pictured the professional gambler as driving a black convertible, wearing a black hat, escorting two gorgeous blondes and tossing money around like Imus Pressit tosses advice.

How wrong can you be? I spend 2½ hours every day driving to Atlantic City and 2½ hours back. It takes me 2-3 hours a day to handicap all of the football, baseball, or basketball games, to come up with one or two lousy decisions.

A Poker game offers the thought that it is a happy exercise, where 7 or 8 guys get together and stuff their guts with goodies while the players take turns telling stories of big wins at other games and tell tales of big nights with beautiful women.

Let me clue you in on a typical Poker game where I attempt to pick up a few dollars. The other players don't make jokes and don't make mistakes.

If you stay too long, or get out too soon or play scared or play stupid, these wolves will gobble your money quicker than a blink.

Talk is minimal, mercy is absent, good hands are scarce and skill is a necessity. Mistakes are expensive and losing nights are very discouraging.

What I am trying to say is that the life of a professional gambler isn't the fun and games that Maverick would lead you to believe.

Being a professional gambler calls for you to have all facets of the Big 4, especially Discipline, and even then, the pro has only a 50-50 chance of winning.

You don't have to be a professional gambler to win but at least take the time to learn the game where you risk your money. Approach gambling the way the pro does.

If you risk money at any form of gambling, be sure you're perfect at that game, be sure you have enough money to compete, be sure you know what to bet after a win and what to bet after a loss.

Finally, be sure you have the driving desire to win, just like the professional does. What the heck do you think I'm asking you to do?

(a) Go without eating for 7 days?

(b) Walk on hot coals?

(c) Not watch TV for three weeks?

(d) Talk nice to your wife?

(e) Throw away the back issues of *Playboy* you have hidden in the garage?

I ain't asking you to do any of these things that will 'cause you grief! I'm asking you to have the guts to practice Discipline like the Professional Gambler and the brains to realize that it's more fun to win small amounts than be entertained for five hours and lose like a jerk.

If the pro can master Discipline, so can you.

9

Wrapping Up Discipline

We come to the end of Discipline but it should be just the beginning of your new attitude and outlook on gambling, with Discipline as the focal point.

In plain simple terms: If you ain't gonna heed the words I've given you about the importance of Money Management and Discipline, you ain't got a prayer of a chance of winning consistently.

A lot of you are gonna put this book down and revert to your old way of playing. Some of you will see the need for Discipline and make some variations off my suggestions. Good!

I don't give a rat's tail what method you use or how you change the Systems, as long as you have some type of control, some semblance of Discipline.

My friend Hope Liss is a very nice girl but a hopeless gambler. She wants so bad to win, but can't be burdened with any type of thinking.

She agrees that she must change her ways in order to have a chance at winning but refuses to take the time to follow my rules. A lot of you are as hopeless as Hope Liss.

You agree that a change is mandatory but can't pull the trigger on getting started on the proper road to smart gambling.

One last time I'll make a list of what you need to gamble sensibly and have a shot at the machines. You'll see The Big Four,

The Little Three, and all the other things I've harped on for pages and pages. One last time, take a good look. Be sure you:

(1) Have a decent **Bankroll**,
(2) Have a complete **Knowledge** of payoffs,
(3) Predetermine a **Money Management** method,
(4) Preset your **Discipline** controls,
(5) Decide on a couple of **Systems** you'll use,
(6) Apply your own **Theory** to the Systems you choose,
(7) Have a **Logical** approach to each System,
(8) Take advantage of hot **Trends**,
(9) Set **Naked Pulls**,
(10) Set **Naked Numbers**,
(11) Set **Win Goals**,
(12) Set **Loss Limits** and follow them,
(13) Break Bankroll into **Sessions**,
(14) Have your **Series** intelligently based on your Session amount,
(15) Play only at machines within your financial structure,
(16) When reach Win Goal, set **Guarantee and Excess**,
(17) If get ahead, be sure you leave with a profit,
(18) If you're losing, wrap it up for that day,
(19) Set small **Percentage Returns**,
(20) **Learn How To Win.**

Money Management and Discipline will change your whole approach to gambling and the crime of it is that only a handful of you realize it.

I guess this wraps up the section on Discipline and only God knows if I've reached any of you. But just let me give you my favorite analogy one more time:

"Seventy percent of the people who enter a casino get ahead. Ninety percent of that seventy percent put the money back into the machines."

Therein lies the scourge of the undisciplined player: No Discipline, or have I said that before?

Odds and Ends

1

Comps

Here's a subject that seems to be on the minds of most people when they enter a casino: "How much you gonna give me in Comps?"

The term *comp* is derived from the word *complimentary,* which in street talk means "something for nuttin."

Many years ago, when Las Vegas first opened, they wanted to get people to keep coming into their casinos and used the giving of meals, rooms, shows as a come-on. The method worked. People got in the habit of looking for comps and even today the casinos heap these "freebies" on their patrons. For instance, all drinks are free in the casinos and people take this gift for granted. But people ain't satisfied with just a few drinks. They think they should be rewarded just for sitting at a table.

My friend I. D. Cerv is a typical sponger in the casinos. I. D. Cerv thinks he deserves top treatment because he is honoring a certain casino with his play.

He walks into a casino, saunters up to a Blackjack table, buys in for $40 and plunks down $5. He loses and immediately calls over the floor person: "Excuse me, sir, any chance of getting a meal for my wife and me?" It's kind of a demand, not a request.

The floor person, trying to stifle a guffaw at the arrogance of this dork, says very politely: "Sir, you have to be rated, based on some extended play. Then we'll be happy to look over your situation."

You'd think he punched I. D. Cerv in the mouth because he refused his silly request. "Hey, Mac, I deserve to be comped. I come to your lousy casino every month and give you all my action. Send over your boss, I'll have your badge for this."

You think this don't happen in a casino? It goes on every day. The casinos do have a comp program and it is very generous in its intent.

The casinos wanna reward their high rollers and heavy players, along with those patrons who show up many many times a month. They have the right to decide who they want to comp.

The intent is to take care of the people who go to the same casino and lay out some heavy bread. I concur wholeheartedly with their actions.

Obviously there is a reasoning for their methods. They wanna reward the strong player who bets heavy and the frequent visitor. They want these people coming back, so they'll have some more shots at beating them.

The casinos know why they do it. The players know why they do it. The players know that the casinos know they know. The casinos know that the players know that the casinos know they know. The players know that the casinos know that they know they know. The casinos know...well, you get the idea.

The casinos have a rating system to comp you, even with slots play. You are rewarded, based on your action. That means:

(a) How long you play,
(b) How often you play,
(c) How much you play.

My opinion is that you should play to win a percentage of

your Bankroll and if you get comped, so be it. If you don't get comped, it ain't like Sophia kicked you in the shins. Just use your profits to buy your own lunch.

Comps can be overrated and expensive. Don't make them the focal point of your day. Positively don't bet higher just to be noticed.

2

Etiquette in a Casino

You think this ain't important? You look around the next time you walk into a casino and see if you don't see people acting like dorks, oblivious to everyone around them.

Some people have one quirk or maybe two, some have three or four, others like Etta Gerk has no etiquette at all. During the course of a day, she'll break 70% of these rules and on a good day will smash them all. Here's what she'll do:

(a) Wait for someone to turn their back at a slot machine and she'll run up and start playing;

(b) Sit at a Blackjack table and blow smoke out of her mouth, her left nostril and her right ear, making sure she hits everybody on both sides;

(c) At the Roulette table she has spilled her drink at 16 consecutive Sessions;

(d) At 8 of those Sessions she had a doubleheader. She knocked over her neighbor's drink, reaching for a far number;

(e) At the Craps table she makes her bet as the dice come out, changing the flow of the dice when cubes hit her hand;

(f) Insults the cocktail waitress for bringing a weak drink (it was free, of course, and she ain't never left a tip in all the time she visits the casinos);

(g) Constantly, I mean continuously, badgers floor people for comps, even though her play does not warrant them;

(h) On busy days, ties up 6 quarter machines at once, while people walk around, looking for Slots to play;

(i) Offers constant advice to people at the machines as to their playing too fast, or too slow, or too many coins or not enough coins. In other words...a pest;

(j) Has the brazen audacity to ask for cigarettes, candy or cookies from strangers, and to borrow money from her traveling companions.

Etta Gerk is a jerk and a pest. Her behavior spares no one. The crazy thing is that people tolerate "gerks" like this, instead of just ignoring them.

I know it's hard to put someone like this in their place, but until they are taught that you ain't gonna tolerate their nonsense, they'll continue their abusive behavior.

The casino personnel put up with people like this every day. They have a saying that encompasses all of these "gerks":

"When a known pest comes through the door,

Don't sink to their level, ignore the bore!"

You'd do well to heed that advice, unless of course you're guilty of a couple of these things. If you are...well, that's another story!

3

Thieves

I could spend hours and chapters describing things that happen in a casino. Not because the casinos are bad places, but because bad people go to places that cater to people.

There are crowds in a casino, all intent on gambling, having a good time, enjoying the action. Their minds are not on the idea that there are people who prey on these distractions to reap the rewards, by stealing from the patrons.

Security in the casinos is excellent but the fact is they can't be everywhere, at every table, at every slot, all day long. That's where you gotta use your own protective measures.

I'd like to relate two stories, both of which happened to my mother, and naturally you can play "Can You Top This?" because you've probably heard or encountered better ones.

One day she was in the ladies room and closed the door of the stall. She hung her pocketbook on the hook that is approximately a quarter of the way from the top of the door of the stall.

When she turned to flush the toilet, a person from the next stall, listening for the right sound, was poised to make their move the instant the flush was started.

A girl came over the separation, leaned down, grabbed the pocketbook off the hook, dropped down on the other side and was gone.

Before my mother could grasp what had happened and

216

opened her door, there was no one in sight. It was a well planned move, obviously done before. She lost EVERYTHING! And I mean everything she had in that pocketbook.

Since women are prone to carry everything with them, the trouble we had replacing cards, glasses, keys, pictures, notes, not to mention the money, was painful and tedious.

Another time she was sitting at a 50¢ machine, a bucket of coins to her right on the stand next to the machine she was playing at. Suddenly something hit her left leg. She turned and on the floor was a half dollar.

She knew it wasn't hers, so she asked the man next to her if he dropped a coin. The man said no, and as she turned back to her machine, her bucket was gone.

An instant! A fraction of a second was all this team needed to make their move. They are pros. They are lice. They are filth who prey upon people who can't fathom that animals like this are not in cages.

These thieves are good at what they do. Before they make their move, they're aware of who has money, who is around, where their escape is, where they can switch to an accomplice and most of all, they have a back-up diversion that is used in case the "mark" turns too soon and catches them in the act.

If my mother did NOT turn to talk to that man and merely looked back to her machine in time to see her thief, another "partner" would have sprung into action, giving time for "slime #1" to get away.

Some work alone, but rarely, because they operate better in teams, and all are experienced. They work on these moves constantly.

You can't stop them, once they spring into action. You can avoid it happening by taking precautions.

The next chapter lays out some of these preventive methods. Before you look at that chapter, think about situations you may have encountered or heard about.

4

Luck in Gambling

One of the most overused words in gambling is that 4-letter powerhouse: Luck. Everybody thinks that luck is gonna determine whether they win or lose on a certain day. What a bunch of poppycock.

Luck has absolutely, positively nothing whatsoever to do with whether you win or lose. Everybody has luck. Sometimes it's good, sometimes bad.

Here are some situations:

(1) You're gonna be at a machine that's hot.
(2) You're gonna be at a machine that's cold.
(3) You're gonna take advantage of Hot Trends.
(4) You ain't gonna take advantage of Hot Trends.
(5) You're gonna stay at a freezing cold machine, even though you're losing.
(6) You're gonna be smart enough to leave a cold machine.
(7) You're gonna quit when you have a nice profit (30% maybe?).
(8) You're gonna get ahead and like a dork pour that money back into the machine.

There ain't no mention of luck in any of those statements. You're either gonna use Discipline and quit while you're ahead, regardless of the amount, or you're gonna bang away all day long, going for the kill.

That ain't luck determining your outcome. It's plain old stupid decisions. It don't take bad luck to give back money that is realistically yours, after you win it.

Yet everyone blames God, or the good fairy or the bad witch, or the sun, or the position of the rays, for whether they win or not.

I gotta tell you how I look at it: When I win, I'm thankful I had the brains to quit with a profit. When I lose, I try to keep the losses down and analyze my moves, which resulted in those losses.

This is what sounds so corny, yet you hear these remarks every day:

(a) I lost because God hates me.

(b) I lost because my wife made me wait and I had nothing else to do.

(c) If luck was a germ, I'd have pneumonia.

(d) Bad luck is my shadow, it follows me to every table.

You don't lose because of bad luck. You lose because you're either a lousy player or you got no Discipline, or the Trend on a certain day was just going against you.

I don't believe in luck. I don't believe that anyone hates me, or that I'm being punished, or that the position of a hot ball of light has any bearing whatsoever on the outcome of my gambling.

Put that crap outta your head about luck. It has no place in gambling. None! Zippo!

You win because of hot Trends, good Money Management and Discipline.

You lose when things are not streaking and you're getting chopped. But mainly you lose because you won't quit with a profit.

No other reason!

5

Intimidation

I ain't never seen Intimidation come more into play than in a casino. People who drive 95 miles an hour on a crowded parkway are scared to walk up to a Blackjack table.

Girls who wear enough clothes to stick under a stamp, become intimidated that someone is looking at them at a Roulette table. (That's not to say they should start changing their dressing arrangements, except maybe to wear less, but that's another story.) But they should also spend more time seeing that there is nothing to fear at these tables.

Guys who play hockey, basketball and football without pads or protection, risking injury to win a meaningless game, are scared to death to walk into a Baccarat pit.

Guys and gals who brave the rigors of diving off a super-high springboard into 10 feet of water, or who dare to drive a new car on any street in Manhattan, are petrified of a Craps table.

Intimidation is the thing that keeps many people from playing the table games and I never could understand why. They hear a couple of loud guys at a table and are afraid some of them might say something to the novice about their style of play or Knowledge of that game.

It amazes me how many people admit this fear. Once they get past this initial fear, everything is okay, but breaking the ice is the problem.

The intimidated player will then turn to the Slots where they can hide. No one questions how they play and no Knowledge is needed to make moves, such as how much you wanna bet, or what plays to make at the table games.

Even though it's snap city to play Craps or Roulette or Baccarat, you still have the Intimidation factor scaring away the players.

I mentioned this factor because it works against the Slots player who would like to play another game. But you play Slots because you're scared to take the shot at games that give you less chance of losing.

I'll bet you're gonna be too intimidated to write down the Series of some of the Systems I told you to use. Or you won't even take a sheet of paper, outlining a betting Series, because you're afraid someone might see you using a System in slots and you'd feel funny. Tsk, Tsk, Tsk.

Think about it! Are you intimidated by the people at the table games? Is that why you play the Slots?

Just like there is no need to think Luck affects you in the casino, Intimidation is something you should avoid. Suck up your gut, swallow twice and jump right up to those tables. There's NOTHING to be scared of. Absolutely NOTHING!

6

A Commercial

While I still have your attention, let's drop in a commercial and maybe you'll read a few lines before slamming the book closed.

It is an explanation of the 7 other books I have written and a brief word or two on each of the 22 video tapes that are already on the market. By the time you read this chapter there may be a couple more videos.

The price of the books are listed and the tapes are 3 for $99 plus $4 handling except for a few that are lower in cost. An address and phone will be shown at the end of the chapter. Everything is entitled, "So You Wanna Be A Gambler."

BLACKJACK ($14.95)
Basic approach to a tough game. Explanation of every type hand, plus Money Management moves.

ROULETTE/SLOTS ($13.95)
Has Systems and explanations on the playing of Slot Machines. Then we swing into the initial approach to Roulette with Systems, Money Management and Discipline.

CRAPS ($19.95)
First book on Craps. Starts at beginning and brings you right

through the Money Management moves. If you're interested in Craps, this will give you insight into the game.

ADVANCED CRAPS ($29.95)
This book is far and away the best book I've ever written. It covers the entire game of Craps with a load of variations and Money Management Theories. It's expensive, but that's because it's so effective in mastering this game. Even if you don't play Craps, the Discipline Theories are very strong.

CARD COUNTING ($19.95)
Counting cards is a snap and this book goes deep into teaching you the moves and shows how you can get to count a deck in 15 seconds. If you play Blackjack, you should count.

ADVANCED ROULETTE ($19.95)
Very strong approach to a good game. Many methods and of course a heavy approach to Money Management and Discipline. Strongly recommend this book, and the one on Card Counting (only if you play Blackjack).

BACCARAT ($14.95)
Best game in the house. Good chance for streaks. Book shows ways of picking up Trends and how to bet them.

Following are the videos and they range in time from one hour to an hour and 15 minutes. As I said, they're all $39.95 each, or 3 for $99, plus postage unless stipulated otherwise.

BASIC BLACKJACK
For the Basic player who is not into Counting.

ADVANCED BLACKJACK
For the Card Counter. Also deep into speed moves and Money Management.

BASIC ROULETTE
For the Basic player. Systems, Discipline, etc.

ADVANCED ROULETTE
Really good approach for a game that is excellent as springboard to table games.

BEGINNER CRAPS
For the newcomer to craps. Explains the game from THE BEGINNING.

INTERMEDIATE CRAPS
Starts to get heavy into methods and Discipline.

ADVANCED CRAPS
This gets deep into hedging and offshoots of Money Management.

SUPER CRAPS
All sorts of hedging and variations of spinoffs.

BACCARAT
Visual look at a game that a monkey could play. Goes into betting systems and Theory.

VIDEO POKER
Strategy for every type of hand you'll get plus betting techniques.

CHARTING TABLES
My pet peeve against gamblers. You gotta chart tables. This tape concentrates on these moves.

PAI GOW POKER
This game is in Las Vegas and Atlantic City. Ranks up there with Baccarat as great game. A super snap to learn.

DRAW POKER
Goes over strategy moves for 5-card draw.

7 CARD STUD
Good look into moves to make from a conservative money-making Theory.

HORSE RACING
For the occasional race goer. How to read charts, handicap, and How to Bet.

COLLEGE FOOTBALL
For the intermediate handicapper. Shows how to apply past game information and Money Management.

PRO FOOTBALL
Good look at handicapping moves, teaser application and mostly betting moves. Stresses getting good work habits.

SLOTS ($24.95)
Mostly concentrates on how to bet, as opposed to just walking up to any machine and playing.

LOTTERY ($24.95)
Guide to number selection methods, and wheeling techniques. Will give you insight into Money Control.

CASINO SURVIVAL KIT ($24.95)
Strictly for the beginner. A look into Craps, Roulette and Blackjack for those just getting involved.

I highly recommend you either learn how to gamble and how to use Discipline or get into a safer sideline like defusing atom bombs, otherwise gambling will eat you alive.

These tapes and books are well worth the price and will teach you how to win.

Number to call for orders:

1-800-345-7017

To order by mail:

John Patrick Productions
P.O. Box 289
Short Hills, NJ 07078

If you have any questions, do not hesitate to contact me by mail or phone: (201) 467-4665.

7

The Ultimate Goal

We have reached the final chapter in a book covering Slot Machines. For those of you still around, I hope you grasped the Reality of Gambling and the need for Money Management and Discipline.

If you've read this book, you'll see that gambling requires a strong Disciplined approach, to reach what I believe is The Ultimate Goal...winning!

Yeah yeah, some of you will still maintain that you gamble for the fun of it, or for excitement, or an outlet. But deep in your mind, you believe "dere's gold in dem thar hills" (slots).

I ain't knocking you for wanting the money. I'm knocking you for not realizing what it takes to get it. And when you do realize it...doing the things necessary to reach that gold (or goal, as I try to gently put it).

The way to the end of the rainbow comes through the sections laid out in this book, and by following the Big 4 and Little 3.

(a) Decide on your Bankroll,

(b) Divide into Sessions (Machines),

(c) Pick several Systems,

(d) Lay out your Series,

(e) Set Win Goals,

(f) Set Loss Limits,

(g) Realize the importance of (e) and (f), or have I said that before?

(h) Set Naked Pulls,

(i) Set Naked Numbers,

(j) When reach Win Goal, go into Guarantee and Excess,

(k) When reach Loss Limit... **QUIT!**

It is possible to win at gambling. Maybe not the telephone number amounts you dream about, but a consistent, conservative percentage return.

Will you listen to me and do the things required for you to reach your Ultimate Goal? I rather doubt it and that's a pity.

But if you ever do grasp the real meaning of gambling and wanna grind out sensible returns, do the things I demand you do, as to Money Management and Discipline.

Hope you enjoyed the book, hope you picked up some profitable suggestions. I wish the very best to you and your family in your personal and gambling endeavors.

Just remember what that dork Ivor Gott has already forgotten to remember:

(1) It ain't how much you win at gambling, it's how little you lose,

(2) Seventy percent of the people who enter a casino get ahead a decent percentage of their Bankroll. **Ninety percent** of that seventy percent give it back!

HAPPY WINNINGS
JOHN PATRICK